THE SECRETS OF
ENDURING LOVE

1 3 5 7 9 10 8 6 4 2

Vermilion, an imprint of Ebury Publishing,
20 Vauxhall Bridge Road,
London SW1V 2SA

Vermilion is part of the Penguin Random House group of companies whose
addresses can be found at global.penguinrandomhouse.com

Copyright © Dr Meg John Barker and Professor Jacqui Gabb 2016
Illustrations © The Open University and ESRC

Dr Meg John Barker and Professor Jacqui Gabb have asserted their rights to
be identified as the authors of this Work in accordance with the Copyright,
Designs and Patents Act 1988

First published by Vermilion in 2016

www.eburypublishing.co.uk

A CIP catalogue record for this book is available from the British Library

ISBN 9781785040238

Printed and bound in Great Britain by Clays Ltd, St Ives PLC

Penguin Random House is committed to a sustainable future for our
business, our readers and our planet. This book is made from Forest
Stewardship Council® certified paper.

CONTENTS

ACKNOWLEDGEMENTS

Jacqui Gabb would like to thank the team of researchers who contributed to the success of the *Enduring Love?* research project. Without their hard work, professionalism and enthusiasm there would be no research evidence to analyse. Especially big thanks to the researchers who completed fieldwork: Martina Klett-Davies, Tam Sanger, Reenee Singh and Danni Pearson. Thanks are also due, here, to Susanna Abse (CEO, Tavistock Centre for Couple Relationships); Penny Mansfield, CBE (Director, oneplusone); Ruth Sutherland (CEO, Relate); Nick Turner (Relate); and Janet Walker, OBE (Relate/University of Newcastle) whose expertise and involvement ensured that our research remained attuned to the needs of couples and families in counselling and relationship support. Eternal thanks go to Janet Fink who was my research collaborator on the project. The quality of the data is in large part down to her sensitivity, thoughtfulness and attention to detail. Janet remains one of the most important people in my life. Personal thanks to my family and friends – one and all.

Meg John would like to thank Jacqui for being so generous in involving me in this wonderful project, and all the people whose conversations during the writing of this book have been so helpful. Particular gratitude goes to Ed and his family for the Boxing Day dinner conversation, and to my Facebook friends for getting so excited discussing their everyday acts of kindness. Also cheers to Amelia and Harri for putting me onto love languages and meta-communication. Thanks so much all for inspiring me and giving me such great examples and ideas to play with.

We'd also both like to express our great appreciation to the Economic and Social Research Council* for funding the

Enduring Love? project, to the Faculty of Social Sciences and all our colleagues at the Open University for their invaluable support, and to everyone at Penguin Random House for their enthusiasm for the project and for their help in putting this book together.

Last but by no means least, a particular debt of gratitude goes to the research participants who generously took part in the study, especially those whose stories are included in this book. There really would be no book without them!

*The ESRC funding code for this project was RES-062-23-3056.

FOREWORD

We all want love to endure. It's the dream we human beings yearn for: a bond that is strong and true and lasts for ever.

And we all know that love demands that we endure. That although loving can be wonderful, sometimes it also means facing harsh and demanding relationship challenges.

Though romance may seem bright and shiny, long-term love is often not easy. It was Erich Fromm – perhaps the most significant commentator on love in modern times – who suggested that while 'falling in love' is the phrase we think of most readily, much more significant is the concept of 'standing in love', being willing to keep going, keep trying, keep caring through time.

Every day – as a relationship coach and an advice columnist – I see people struggling to keep 'standing', to create enduring love in their own lives. I see how much people want to succeed in their relationships, how much they want knowledge and understanding to help them stay the course.

Where better to gain this knowledge than by learning from others? What's needed is an accurate, careful, well-executed piece of research showing us how ordinary people actually do make love work. Which is why the Open University *Enduring Love?* research project is so vital. What's also needed is an inspiring, helpful, well-written book showing us how to put into practice the lessons of that research. Which is why *The Secrets of Enduring Love* – written by Meg John Barker and Jacqui Gabb – is so important.

The book's not just important because it is fascinating, though it is. Nor because it offers proven evidence on the one hand, and debunks unhelpful myths on the other, which it does. This book is also important because every page contains practical guidance on how we can all make our relationships the best they can be.

Whether you have a partnership or are searching for one, whether you are in in the initial stage of rose-coloured glasses or a little way down the line when the glasses (and even the gloves) are off, this book will be both entertaining and useful.

Read it from cover to cover. Then dip back into it to deepen your understanding, inspire your commitment or to find support when crisis strikes. It explains, reveals, advises and guides. It will reassure you by showing that most couples hit difficulties, then encourage you by showing that despite this, many couples fully succeed in trusting, sharing, supporting and cherishing.

Because above all, *The Secrets of Enduring Love* is a hopeful book. It offers hope not only to each of us individually but also to society as a whole. It proves beyond doubt that despite all humankind's hesitation, confusion, fear and cynicism, despite all the jibes of the mass media and despite all the challenges of modern living, human love is alive and well.

When we read *The Secrets of Enduring Love*, we realise fully – and with optimism – that in the twenty-first century, love does indeed endure.

Susan Quilliam

INTRODUCTION

Why This Book?

'And they lived happily ever after.' From fairy tales to Hollywood movies, we all know that any good love story ends this way. Just as the relationship starts, the story stops. But what happens after 'happily ever after'? This book is all about exactly that: how you can live your life, day-to-day, over the whole of your relationship.

There's a lot of advice out there about relationships: self-help books, problem pages, and websites all promising you 'the secret of staying together', the rules for 'keeping your love alive', or 'the answer to overcoming relationship problems'. But not much of the advice is based on real-life experience. That's why we carried out a research study with over five thousand people in long-term relationships. We wanted to find out what they were actually *doing* to make their relationships work, so that we could share their secrets with you.

In this book we've brought together the findings of that study with what we know from other research on love, and from relationship therapy, to give you the low-down on how to make relationships last.

All the way through we've included stories from the people we spoke to so you can see how it works in reality. We're deeply grateful to them for sharing their experiences with us so generously, even the hard parts. When you read all the different ways they've found of sustaining their relationships, navigating the tough stuff, and celebrating the good times, we think you'll agree that they're the *real* relationship experts. And in the same way, you are the expert on your own relationships. The point of this book is to give you all the ideas, examples, and practical tips that you need to find your own way to enduring love.

Why secrets?

Why have we called this book the *secrets* of enduring love rather than just the *secret*? Well, when you ask people what they do to maintain their relationships, they give lots and lots of different answers. Try asking some of your own friends, family and colleagues and you'll probably find the same thing. Often, what works for one relationship is different to what works for another.

For example, one person says that it means a lot when their partner wakes them up with breakfast in bed every morning. Another person grimaces and says they'd hate that because they need at least an hour alone before they're capable of human contact. One person talks about the importance of having separate interests, another focuses on spending as much time as possible together. One says it's all about talking things through until they're resolved, another says they've learnt when it's best to walk away from an argument.

There are plenty of books out there claiming to have the 'secret' of long-term relationship success: often a list of five or seven rules that will make your relationship last. Those kinds of books promise that anybody who follows their advice will end up with a better relationship.

There certainly *are* things that help to nurture and sustain relationships, but they're definitely not the *same* things for every relationship. The key message you'll find in this book is that different things work for different people, and at different times over the course of their relationship. We found again and again, that different people prioritised different approaches or managed their relationships in different ways.

So you won't find one secret recipe for success in this book, but instead you'll hear about the many *different* things that people do which work so well for them. We'll help you to recognise the small things that you're already doing but which often go unnoticed, and we'll offer you a helping hand to figure out what else might work for you and to put it into practice.

Why enduring love?

We called our project Enduring Love? because we were interested in long-term relationships, but also because we want to capture the fact that long-term relationships can be a positive or a negative thing in people's lives – and everything in between.

The word 'enduring' has two possible meanings: it can mean long-lasting, or it can mean patiently tolerating something that is usually painful and prolonged. Love can be something that's valuable because it 'endures' over time, but it can also feel like something that has to be 'endured' when times get tough in relationships. Sometimes relationships can even feel like something of an 'endurance test'.

So we need to be clear, up front, that this book isn't saying that any one way of doing relationships is the *right way*. A lot of the time, when we talk about our research, people ask us whether a certain kind of relationship can be 'successful'. They say things like 'can people who live apart have a successful relationship?' or 'can couples who aren't monogamous have a successful relationship?' Generally we answer these kinds of question with another question: 'what do you mean by "successful"?' This often catches people out a bit, because they haven't thought about that! After all, everybody knows what a successful relationship looks like, right? The answer they generally come up with is that success means lasting long-term.

Actually we're not saying that long-term relationships are any better, or more successful, than any other kind. You only have to think of a relationship where people have stayed unhappily together to know that long-term isn't necessarily a good thing. In our research we spoke to many people who'd had more than one relationship over the course of their lives and it was clear that relationships that ended could also be successful. They could be wonderful while they lasted, and also good when they ended. Some turned into great friendships or positive co-parenting arrangements, for example. Some ended painfully. Whatever the ending, people often felt that they'd learnt a lot from these past relationships and were determined to take 'lessons learnt' into the rest of their lives.

Even though we did focus on long-term relationships, you'll also see that 'long term' means very different things to different people. For younger people it might mean six months, whereas for others it has to be more than a decade to count as long term. For some it's about how long they've been together, for others it's more about how they imagine their future together.

Even though the focus in this book is on long-term relationships, we're not saying that these are somehow better than being single, for example, or than having shorter-term relationships. One thing you'll find in this book is that people are doing their relationships in all sorts of different ways. Some people live together and some people don't. Some have children and others don't. Some are with a partner of a different gender and some of the same gender. Some are in their first relationship while others are second-, third- or fourth-time-rounders. Some are monogamous, some are non-monogamous, and some are something in between. Some people prioritise a partner above all other people in their lives whereas others see their partner relationship as one among many others.

It's clear that there are as many different ways of doing relationships as there are people, and all of these ways have their own challenges and rewards, their own possibilities and pitfalls. In our study we specifically made sure that we spoke to people of all different ages, classes and cultural backgrounds, as well as people in different kinds of relationships and families. So, over the course of this book, you'll probably find some relationships that seem very familiar to you and others that feel very different. But hopefully you can learn something from all of them, and from the different people who're finding their own ways towards lasting relationships.

The words we've used

Just as there are many different kinds of relationships, people also use lots of different words to talk about the people they have relationships with. Some refer to spouses, husbands or wives, others to girlfriends or boyfriends. Through the book we've generally used the word 'partner' as a pretty neutral term to cover these different words, unless we're actually quoting a specific person, in which case we've used whatever words they use themselves.

Similarly, although most of the people we studied saw themselves as 'couples', here we usually use the word 'relationship' because that also includes people whose relationships have more than two people in them. You'll read more about this in Chapter 5.

Who are we?

So who are we to be writing this book? Basically this book is a collaboration between one of the main researchers on the Enduring Love? project (Jacqui) and a relationship writer and therapist (Meg John). Both of us have been researching and writing about families and relationships for many years now.

In this book we've combined our skills to bring you the findings of the research, weaving them together with other useful ideas from relationship therapy, in a way that'll be helpful for your own relationships.

Reading This Book

Whatever your reason for picking this book up there's something in it for you. If you're generally interested in the topic of relationships then you can read the content and skip over the suggested activities. If you're looking for more of a self-help book, then we've pulled out a lot of ideas, quizzes, tips and activities, which you can try out yourself. You can even use the book as a kind of workbook, spending a week on each chapter – for example – and trying out all of the suggestions. You could read the book alone or share it with a partner, completing the activities together and talking through the questions.

It's also up to you how you read the book. It's fine to read it cover-to-cover, but we've also written it so that each chapter, and each section within each chapter, stands on its own. So it's fine to dip into whatever interests you most rather than reading it in any particular order. Where there are connections between the chapters, we've included links backwards and forwards throughout the book, which you can follow if you like.

What next?

Through the rest of the book, we'll take you on a journey through various different aspects of relationships, drawing out what people said in our study, and exploring what might work for you.

Here's a quick overview of what's covered in each chapter to help you find your way from here:

CHAPTER 1: EVERYDAY KINDNESS

One main thing that came out of the research was the huge importance of moments of kindness in relationships. People feel valued when their partner makes small gestures to show that they're thinking of them. People also love it when their partner expresses their gratitude when they do something for them. In Chapter 1 we explore how you can weave kindness and appreciation into your own relationships. We also cover how to make time for your relationship in an increasingly hectic and demanding world, and the importance of having both time together and separate 'me-time'.

CHAPTER 2: ON THE HOME FRONT

We found that home is really important, being the place where our relationships often actually happen. However, these days we live in lots of different kinds of set-ups: sometimes together and sometimes apart. In Chapter 2 we explore how you can use your home to nurture your relationship, and also how our relationships play out in different parts of the home. We'll help you think through how you can make space for togetherness and separateness, as well as identifying your comfort zones, and hot spots.

CHAPTER 3: IT'S NOT WHAT YOU SAY...

Experts often say that communication is the most vital thing in a relationship. We found that being able to talk to each other certainly was helpful, but silence was often just as valuable. In Chapter 3 we cover forms of spoken *and* non-verbal communication, like the shared smile or the knowing glance. We look at how online communication can both endanger *and* enrich your relationship, and we cover how to communicate in times of relationship conflict. We also explore how to bring laughter into your relationship, and how to communicate about how you like to communicate!

CHAPTER 4: LET'S TALK ABOUT SEX

Another thing that experts often say is vital to a relationship is sex. Some go so far as to claim that it's the glue that holds relationships together. Actually this is a myth. Like other research, we found that people prioritise many other aspects of relationships over sex. In Chapter 4 we cover how you can make space for physical intimacy of lots of different kinds, as well as how to navigate the impact of parenting, body changes, and other shifts over time, on sex and desire.

CHAPTER 5: THE MAGIC NUMBER

Something that's key in a relationship is having some kind of 'third element' to help keep it stable: like the third leg on a stool. Chapter 5 explores the role these third elements might have for you. We consider the impact of children, something that will be of particular interest to parents, and pets, for those of you who are animal lovers. We also look at the role of religion and beliefs, interests and pastimes. Crucially we consider the importance of friendship, and other relationships, for supporting you and your relationship.

CHAPTER 6: YOUR LOVE STORY

The last chapter of the book explores how you can navigate your own real relationships when there are so many idealised love stories in the world around you. How important is saying 'I love you', and what does it even mean? How can you tell your own relationship story, when this goes against the grain? And what happens when major events and transitions occur in our lives, forcing our relationship stories to change?

We do hope that you enjoy reading the book as much as we enjoyed writing it.

Meg John Barker & Jacqui Gabb

CHAPTER 1

EVERYDAY KINDNESS

No act of kindness, no matter how small, is ever wasted.

– Aesop

I f you ask yourself what makes a relationship last, you'll probably automatically think of the big things: how we communicate about important issues, how we manage conflict, or how we cope when a major crisis hits. All these are covered in this book, but we aren't starting there. That's because what came across loud and clear in our research was that, when it comes to enduring love, it's the everyday small stuff that matters.

Before going any further, have a think about this:

QUIZ TIME: FEELING APPRECIATED AND VALUED

Note down two things that a partner could do for you that would make you feel appreciated or valued. If you're in a relationship at the moment you could say what your partner actually does. If not, think back to a previous relationship, or think what you'd most like a partner to do.

1. _____

2. _____

Being appreciated and valued by a partner makes people feel good about their relationships. It also helps them to weather the storms when things get difficult. The psychologist John Gottman found that people in happy relationships had a higher ratio of kind comments to harsh ones compared with those in unhappy relationships, showing how important everyday kindness is.

In fact, based on his research, Gottman came up with what he called a 'magic ratio'. Relationships that lasted over time had *five times* as many appreciative interactions as they did critical ones. It didn't much matter how much conflict there was in the relationship. Some were relatively calm and others were quite fiery. What mattered was that the moments of valuing each other far outweighed the moments of nagging or niggling. Think about your own relationships. Do you say positive things five times as many times as you do negative ones?

We wanted to see what this kind of valuing and appreciation actually *looks like* in people's relationships. Here are the top five answers given by people in our survey.

VITAL STATISTICS:

What do partners do to make you feel appreciated?

Top five answers:

- Thoughtful gifts and kind gestures
- Saying 'thank you' and noticing my accomplishments
- Sharing the household chores and/or childcare
- Talking with me and listening to me
- Physical affection such as cuddles or foot massage

We'll cover the last three of these in more detail in later chapters, but it's worth noticing that all of these answers emphasise small everyday activities: doing chores together, listening to somebody's day, or having a cuddle. Relationship advice often focuses on big talks and great sex, but people actually find that everyday chats and little signs of affection are more meaningful.

In this chapter we'll explore the top two answers in more depth. You'll learn more about what thoughtful gestures look like and how you can show your appreciation for each other. We'll also cover how we can be kind to both ourselves and our partners in our relationships.

Thoughtful gestures: it starts with a cup of tea

Many people told us about the importance of little everyday acts of kindness in sustaining their relationship. And by far the most common example they gave? Being brought a cup of tea! For example people said things like:

'What does my partner do to make me feel appreciated? Makes me tea! No really, it's the little things.'

'I always leave a mug near the kettle for him with a tea bag inside. I know that he can do this himself, but it's nice to do it.'

'The lovely cup of tea with biscuits: we do a lot of that. We like sharing the tea in the morning, it's a way we relax. He knows I don't do mugs at all, so I've got a cup and saucer and he's got a mug. If everything's in the dishwasher he'll wash up a cup and saucer for me. I'm quite spoilt.'

These are just a few examples, but tea was mentioned so frequently in our project that we had to put it in a category all of its own!

Obviously the focus on tea has a lot to do with the fact that we focused on the UK: a cuppa is a British cultural icon. But we've checked with people in other countries and we've found that thoughtful gestures are important wherever you are.

Bringing a partner a hot beverage is a common gesture in many places, but we also heard about the importance of packing an intricate lunchbox in Japan, of warming up the car on a cold morning in Canada, and of going out in the rain to buy bread rolls in Germany. In Malawi it's generally better to give a loved one a fish than a bunch of flowers. In Alaska women leave the toilet seat up as a kind gesture for male partners, reversing the etiquette that is commonly found in the UK and US.

Of course all of these things differ between people in the same culture as well as between different cultures. People of different classes or different religious faiths also have different little rituals for example. For example, several people told us about the importance of their partner deciding to fund a 'night off' cooking because they were tired, but there were class differences in whether this meant their partner went 'down the chippy' (for the British classic of fish and chips), 'ordered takeaway', or took them for a 'posh nosh' meal in a favourite local restaurant. We heard about the importance of saying grace together before meals for some Christian people, and how the loss of this ritual was very difficult when one person lost their faith. Others spoke of praying or meditating together, having separate rituals for this according to gender, or walking quietly around a partner who was doing so when they didn't share the same faith. Importance was also placed on sharing specific meals or religious festivals together, or going to specific places on the summer and winter solstice for pagan partners.

Age is also crucial here: what works in your fifties isn't the same as what works in your twenties, and having children – or not – also makes a difference to what you appreciate.

Think about which thoughtful gestures are most meaningful in your culture or community. Which are most meaningful to you personally? Would you want the same kinds of gestures now as you did ten years ago?

Considerate acts

To give you some further ideas of what kinds of thoughtful gestures might be useful in your own relationships, the classic cup of tea was often combined with another common practice: that of bringing a partner breakfast in bed.

> *'A cup of tea in bed every now and again makes you feel so appreciated.'*

> *'He takes the kids out without me, brings me a cup of tea in bed in the mornings.'*

Obviously kindness from a partner is a great way to start the day. This is particularly the case for parents. The people who do the lion's share of the childcare really appreciate a bit of time out.

People who're very busy with work, inside or outside the home, also really like considerate acts at the end of the working day. For example, Duncan said:

> *'It's a nice feeling to know that if she had a bad day or a long day I'm able to make that a little bit easier, even if it's just having a cup of tea ready when she comes in.'*

Other people spoke about partners who *give me time to relax when I get home from work* or *take out the bins and always clear up after dinner*. Whether it's a partner running a hot bath for us, getting our favourite TV programme set up, or taking the dog out in bad weather, small gestures of everyday kindness are the key, particularly gestures which make a partner's life just that little bit easier:

> *'If he is first in the bathroom before we go to bed he puts the toothpaste on my toothbrush for me.'*

> *'He folds the laundry (which I hate to do).'*

You can see from all of these examples that ordinary, everyday things are often the most meaningful in relationships. There are several reasons for this. One is that we tend to spend much of our lives mulling over the past or planning for the future, often caught up in worries and concerns. Little moments like the ones we've described can help to bring you back to the present and help you to shrug off your cares and worries for a moment.

Kind gestures are important because we also tend to spend much of our time being quite critical of ourselves: doubting our abilities, worrying about our appearance, or questioning our decisions, for example. Small kindnesses from a partner can be a good everyday reminder that we *are* an okay person and that we don't need to be quite so hard on ourselves.

Of course, if it is our partners who are giving us these little moments of presence and kindness in our lives then we're likely to associate them particularly with feeling that sense of stress relief, generosity to ourselves, and joyfulness at noticing those small moments of happiness that are so easy to miss. The more we cultivate this kind of time in our relationships, the greater the positive impact.

TOP TIP

If you have a partner – or somebody else who you spend a lot of your daily life with – try taking one day to deliberately noticing the very small things that they do for you, and that you do for them. Let them know that you're grateful for these specific things. It's easy to start to take these kinds of things for granted, so it's helpful to remind yourself about them from time to time.

The personal touch

People definitely appreciate having thoughtful gestures tailored to them personally, rather than their partner trying to apply some kind of one-size-fits-all version of kindness. Gestures of this kind show someone that they're understood; that you're invested in *this* relationship. For example, with the cup of tea it's all about knowing exactly when it's needed and preparing it just the way the other person likes it.

Nothing works for everybody. Someone who prefers not to eat in the mornings wouldn't appreciate breakfast in bed. A person who works from home might use getting a cup of tea as an opportunity to get up and move around, so however well intentioned they wouldn't really appreciate their partner bringing one to them at their desk. Somebody who prefers showers wouldn't want to have a bath run for them.

It's also interesting that most of us value something personal far more highly than we do an expensive present or a grand gesture. We heard less about bouquets of flowers, posh meals out, or boxes of chocolates than we did about small acts of thoughtfulness, such as someone sending their partner a text message when they knew they had a difficult meeting at work, somebody picking up their partner's favourite magazine when they did the shopping, or someone saving the last sweet in the packet for their partner.

This answer particularly stuck with us: '*Every year he brings me an orange rose from a garden that he maintains.*'

The fact that this man invested time and energy in growing the rose himself made it unique. And the ritual of him presenting this 'first picked' rose to his partner every year made it far more meaningful than any bought gift could ever be.

Another person got their partner a stuffed toy guinea pig because she loved guinea pigs and couldn't have a real one in the rented flat where she lived. Time and time again people emphasised the thought behind the gift. If you switched the gifts around, swapping the orange rose for the stuffed guinea pig, for example, it simply wouldn't work. In fact it would probably have a negative effect – demonstrating *how very little* the partner knew about you and the relationship.

Think about whether you have special treats that you always give your loved one at a certain time of year, or whether you could take an extra moment to leave a loving message somewhere that you know they'll find it.

'He writes me love messages on post-it notes.'

'She leaves little cards for me to find that say nice things on them.'

For some people, thoughtful gifts became part of the whole family culture rather than just something they shared with their partner. For example, when Anish and Arundhati talked about how they expressed love, they spoke about receiving gifts from their daughter, Aiswari. Anish said:

'You don't have to give something expensive. Small things really matter. For example, Aiswari got everyone into her room and she said "I'm going to give everyone a gift". And she gave one poppy to her brother; one poppy to herself. She gave Anish some stickers from her sticker book, and she gave me a leaf.'

The element of surprise

Another thing that lots of people particularly enjoy is a surprise. In our culture we can put a lot of pressure on specific events like Valentine's Day, anniversaries, birthdays and so on. We often expect that partners will give us presents and treats on such occasions. But often the gifts we prize most highly are the unexpected ones, the 'I saw this and thought of you' variety. These confirm that we're in our partner's thoughts on a daily basis, rather than just when a special event comes around.

The element of surprise is also important with thoughtful gestures. People often value them highly because they aren't expected.

'Surprising me with such things as a nice bath, cuppa, favourite TV show or film at just the right time.'

But when it comes to surprises it's important to remember that different things work for different people. Some of us would love to come home to find that our partner has cooked us a romantic meal; others really wouldn't. Some people just don't like surprises. Some would prefer a surprise that wasn't food-related – if they're on a diet, for example. Some of us would struggle to relax over a romantic meal with a partner who'd spent all afternoon preparing the food but had left the house untidy and the kitchen now resembling a demolition site.

So different thoughtful gestures work in different relationships. We can't just apply what works for one person to another, it needs to be personal. Out of the examples we've covered, think about what works best for you, and how you'd go about letting a partner know that, as well as how you might find out what they prefer.

Saying it with words

Words are important as well as gifts and gestures. Certainly most of us like to hear a partner say 'I love you'. Those three little words are often shorthand for affirming our closeness and reassuring us about the strength of the relationship.

However, as you've seen, saying 'I love you' isn't one of the top five ways in which we found that people felt appreciated and valued by their partner. The words that people mentioned much more often were 'thanks' and 'thank you'. We'll return to words of love in Chapter 6, and words more generally in Chapter 3. For now let's think some more about words of gratitude.

The importance of 'thanks'

In a way, gratitude is the other side of the coin of the everyday gifts and thoughtful gestures that we've just been talking about. It means a lot to be acknowledged for the thought and effort we've put into giving a present, or into doing something kind for a partner.

'She notices things I have done and thanks me for doing them.'

People said it was particularly important to be recognised, by their partners for the time and energy they put into the kinds of mundane everyday tasks that often underpin relationships, like domestic chores, or staying in touch.

It's difficult to ensure an exactly equal division of labour between partners, and relationships often do end up with one person doing more of the work in certain areas. However, it makes a big difference to have that effort appreciated, rather than it being taken for granted. For example, Theo said that he didn't mind the fact that he and his partner had different priorities when it came to tidiness. But he did feel resentful if the time and energy that he spent cleaning the house passed by unnoticed.

'Occasionally I'm exhausted and that turns into anger at Emmie, because Emmie does very, very little cleaning beyond bits of the kitchen and so on because she's just not as bothered by it as I am. And that sometimes turns over into resentment that I feel I'm making the place a better environment for her and she's showing no gratitude for it.'

Theo and Emmie's situation is a little unusual because research shows that women generally do the majority of the housework when they live with male partners. Men also often overestimate the amount of housework that they do, whereas women tend to underestimate their contribution.

There was a sense in our study that most of the men who lived with female partners did take for granted that their partner would do more of the work around the house, including both domestic chores, and childcare if they had kids. In these situations men didn't always show much gratitude for the time and effort that their partners put in. They were more likely to express appreciation only when they felt *personally* supported by what their partner did. For example, as one father said: *'She looks after me... washing up, cooking, etc.'*

Women with male partners, on the other hand, generally expressed appreciation for anything that their partners did around the house. They were more likely to notice and appreciate small amounts of household chores and childcare. This is probably due to the common assumption which many people still have that such things are really 'women's work'.

It's helpful for people in all kinds of relationships to think about what they assume, and what they express appreciation for, when it comes to mundane work. If you're in a relationship, think about who does most of the housework, or looks after any children or animals, or provides emotional or practical support. Do you think that your partner feels appreciated or taken for granted? What could you do to make them feel more appreciated? We'll say a lot more about how to have conversations about this kind of thing in Chapter 3.

Saying it or showing it?

Some people feel that *showing* gratitude is just as important as saying it. For example, one person said that their partner *'thanks me for cooking and eats it even if it is awful!'* Again, people have different preferences in how they like gratitude to be expressed. Some of us would only want to be thanked for cooking if our partner actually enjoyed it. Others would rather our partner ate whatever culinary disasters we served up and were grateful for the time and effort that went into them, however bad the outcome!

Appreciation often goes beyond the individuals in the relationship. Several people said it meant a lot when their partner expressed their appreciation of them to friends and family, rather than just to them in private. For example, one person said it was important that their partner: *'Says nice things to me, says nice things about me to others.'*

Many parents said that it was important that their partner encouraged their children to appreciate the love and labour that they put into them. This was especially true for mums. One said she appreciated that her partner, *'Tells the children they have a great mother!'*

As we saw with Anish and Arundhati before, a culture of thoughtful gestures, and appreciation of them, can be something that a whole family, friendship group, or community can foster, not just an individual partnership. These wider support networks can be crucial in supporting relationships, as we'll see in Chapters 5 and 6.

Psychologists have shown that our happiness is strongly linked to feeling gratitude. They've found – for example – that we feel happier if we write letters of gratitude to people we're thankful to, or if we list three things that we feel grateful for at the end of each day. Similar rituals are also good for relationships, such as thanking your partner every time they've done a particular task, or after you've just had a tough conversation together. You could share a couple of things you're grateful for at the end of every day, or make a point of leaving them a thank-you note once in a while. Think about what rituals of gratitude you'd like to develop in your own relationships.

Praise and compliments

As well as words of gratitude and appreciation, many people said that praise and compliments from partners were important to them. This could be praise for a job well done, or a compliment on their appearance.

'He still thinks I'm attractive (and tells me so) after 32 years of marriage.'

You can see here the distinction between something being taken for granted compared with it being appreciated. It's easy in relationships where you see each other every day to stop commenting upon your partner's appearance, or even to fall into making negative rather than positive comments.

Change happens to us all over time, and perhaps none more so than changes in our ageing bodies. For women especially, where being young is seen as so synonymous with beauty, positive comments from a partner can feel very affirming. Showing that you love your partner's gradual tide of grey hair, increasing curves, or the results of gravity, can go a long way to counteract the negative cultural messages surrounding ageing.

The personal touch is also important here. The compliments that people value most highly are often those which explicitly acknowledge the unique qualities that they bring to the relationship.

'Tells me how much he loves and appreciates me not only for what I do for our family but for being who I am and loving him the way I do.'

The kinds of thoughtful gestures that we covered before are bound together with the words of appreciation that we're talking about here. One person does something that makes their partner's life easier and their partner shows how much they appreciate it. Another person says something thoughtful and they're thanked for it. It's an ongoing process of give and take which – over time – bonds us closer together, especially when grounded in closeness and mutual understanding.

This leads us to another theme that will come up again and again throughout this book: reciprocation.

Reciprocating: give and take

One reason that some partners stop saying thank you or making thoughtful gestures over time is that they feel these aren't being reciprocated: it can seem like you're pushing against the tide when you're the only one making the effort.

This was clearly the case for Theo in his resentment towards Emmie when she didn't appreciate the time he spent making their home clean and tidy.

However a feeling of inequality can also sometimes come about not because someone is being thoughtless or ungrateful, but rather because the way they're expressing their gratitude isn't what *you* are looking for. For example, in Theo's case, rather than actually saying 'thank you', it might be that Emmie expresses her gratitude in kind – by doing some other household chore. It could be that the problem for this couple is more to do with miscommunication than inequality.

There's a useful idea here from relationship author Gary Chapman that he called 'love languages'. He points out that different people prefer to have love expressed in different ways. If you look back to the 'vital statistics' box from earlier, you'll see that these five 'languages' are quite similar to the five findings of our research. They are: gifts, words, doing things for each other, quality time and touch.

So you might be the type of person who feels most loved and appreciated when you receive the kinds of thoughtful gestures that we discussed before. Or it might be more important to you to be thanked or told 'I love you'. It could be that you feel most loved when your partner has done the chores or gone to fetch some shopping. Perhaps having specific time carved out to spend together is crucial for you, or maybe it's physical closeness that's the most important thing in your relationship.

Because different people have different preferences it can be a good idea to have a conversation about this. It's so easy to assume that our partner will be the same as us. You could spend years showering them with gifts only to find that it's cuddles that they're craving. You could say 'I love you' several times a day, only to realise that – for them – it's actions that speak louder than words. The singer Billy Bragg captures the differences well in one of his songs. A partner says to him, after an argument, 'no amount of poetry could mend this broken

TRY IT YOURSELF: LOVE LANGUAGES

Number the five examples listed below from 1 to 5 in order of how important they are for you to receive (1 = most important, 5 = least important). Think about which ones make you feel most loved and appreciated. These are not the only possibilities so feel free to add others. For example, having a partner express an interest in your favourite hobby or football team might be really important to you, or having them make public displays of affection, or reacting in just the way you need when you're having a bad time or feeling sad. You can add those kinds of things in the blank spaces. The number of 'love languages' isn't fixed at five!

When you've done this, try redoing the exercise, but this time numbering the same things in order of which ones you find most comfortable doing *for* a partner (1 = most comfortable, 5 = least comfortable).

It might be that there are differences in the way you prefer to give love and the way you prefer to receive it.

- Gifts and gestures
- Words of gratitude, love and appreciation
- Acts of service such as doing chores
- Spending quality time together
- Touch and physical affection
- _____
- _____
- _____

heart, but you can put the hoover round if you want to make a start'. Clearly she values help around the house more highly than clever song lyrics!

There's room for compromise here. Perhaps you can't offer to give public displays of affection to your partner because you find them too embarrassing, even though that's what they prefer. But you could offer to give them a foot massage in the evening in the privacy of your own home, if that's their second most favourite thing to receive.

It's helpful to check in about these things every now and again in a relationship, because they change over time as well. Maybe physical contact becomes too painful during an illness, or sharing household chores becomes more important once young children come along.

Making us-time

When our lives are hectic and full it can be easy for everyday acts of kindness and appreciation to tail off. To counteract this, many people spoke about the importance of creating some 'us-time' in their lives. It's during 'us-time' when the sorts of things we've just been talking about can happen: thoughtful gestures can be given, and received with appreciation.

'We make time to do nice things together that we both enjoy.'

'What I like most is spending time together and sharing these experiences.'

For example, Jennie said that she was grateful to her partner for cooking on the night that they set aside each week for one another, and that was also the time when he'd surprise her with a little gift such as her favourite chocolate bar or a bottle of Coke.

Carving out space for us-time

Some people, like Jennie and her partner, make a specific time each week to spend together: whether that's a day off that they set aside, or a 'date night' which they keep sacred. Relationship advice often recommends date nights as a way of continuing to appreciate each other in long-term relationships. For example, in her diary Genevieve wrote:

'For a couple of months now Jo and I have been trying to do 'date night' once a week. This is where we assign a night, often Thursday from around eight or nine, to have distraction-free time (no mobiles/laptops etc.). We watch a DVD or something relaxing and enjoyable on the TV, sometimes have a bath, and then go to bed in a relaxed mood with the hope that it leads to more... (not always but it often does). This has really helped us as a couple – to make sure we have that quality relaxed time together each week and to keep the flame alive, so to speak!'

We'll cover the idea of keeping desire alive in Chapter 4 because this was part of the reason behind a date night for some people. For others it was just a way to ensure some time away from daily routines when they could enjoy each other's company.

'It's hard to make time to be with each other with children and work commitments.'

Most parents said that it was important to have occasional moments that were just for them, even if this wasn't as formal as a date night. So Arundhati and Anish, who we met earlier, had time on weeknights after their children went to bed, and a ritual of sharing tea together at the weekend. Christy and Thomas had teenagers, which made it hard for them to have evening time alone together. Instead of date nights, they spoke of grabbing a coffee or taking a short stroll with each other. Other people found themselves making time to walk the dog together or chatting last thing at night before going to sleep.

Again a key point here is that different things work for different people, and at different times in the relationship.

Consider whether you have a preference for explicitly agreed time with your partner like date nights or holidays. Or maybe you prefer the kind of everyday contact such as grabbing a cuppa and catching up in those rare and stolen moments in a busy day. Perhaps it's a bit of both.

When Jake and his partner Jeff were asked what made their relationship work, Jake talked about their special *and* ordinary time together, with an emphasis on the latter.

> 'It's a hard thing to describe, but you know it when you see it. It's you being the person that I want to have around when I'm watching DVDs with a crashing headache on a Sunday morning. It's you being the person that I want to do things with, whether that's going to the symphony, or staying at home and watching DVDs, or drinking too much and having a ridiculous conversation that spirals out of control. I want to do that with you.'

As you'll see in Chapters 2 and 4, the theme of watching movies or TV series together – which Genevieve and Jake both spoke about – was mentioned a lot. Perhaps this is because it ticks so many boxes in terms of us-time. It's a relaxing activity which partners can share, and it often gives us an opportunity for some physical closeness too.

Turning time together into us-time

As well as snatching shorter moments together, some busy people turn activities that might be regarded as chores into us-time. By sharing these activities instead of doing them separately, and by bringing an element of fun into them, they become us-time as much as going out for a meal or watching a DVD.

The kinds of activities which lend themselves to this are things like trips to the shops, which could include buying treats or tagging on time in a cafe. Also household chores like decorating can be playful, as well as creating a comfortable space to enjoy together.

However, by far the most common chore that was mentioned in this way was cooking. In fact, many people didn't even see cooking in the same category as other domestic chores because they found it such a relaxing or enjoyable activity. Clearly cooking – for many of us – is a very real way of feeding our relationship.

'We share our love of food, interest in cooking.'

Again different things work for different people. Some people love to cook together, some hate to share the kitchen, and everything in between. Magdalena and her partner take turns cooking but also make it into an us-time activity: a time for demonstrating their care about each other's tastes and preferences.

'We don't cook together but we'll be there together sometimes. If he's cooking or I'm cooking we'll be talking: we'll just be in the kitchen together because we don't like to spoil each other's food! I get fussy if someone does the wrong thing in my food and he's the same.'

We did our research during the global recession, so many people were struggling financially. This was probably another reason for the emphasis on cooking at home. For example, Eleri said:

'We're going out less and we're trying to be careful. But it's not a massive hardship because we have a nice time anyway. What's the difference: cook in or go out? It's still nice. It's still us doing nice things.'

As with the other things we've covered in this chapter, some people turn the shared 'nice thing' of cooking into a whole family or friendship-group activity, especially around celebration times like holidays or weddings. For example, Magdalena and her partner invite a friend round to join them because she has nowhere else to go for Christmas. Together with their family they all spend hours cooking everyone's favourite foods. They nurture their relationship through the medium of food, within a network of other relationships.

Think about the role of cooking and eating in your own relationship. Is it something you do together or separately? Do you have specific roles or do you take turns? Could cooking and eating be something you turn into a kind of 'us-time', or are there other kinds of everyday activities that you'd like to do in that way?

TOP TIP

Think of a daily activity or chore that you usually do alone which could be shared with a partner, friend or family member. You could choose cooking a meal or baking a cake or biscuits, or perhaps something like clearing out a cupboard, doing some gardening, shopping, walking the dog, or taking things to the tip. Make a time to do this together rather than on your own. Beforehand think together about what could make it enjoyable and give it enough time so it doesn't feel rushed. Afterwards reflect on what it was like to turn this activity into 'us-time'.

This all brings us back to our first theme of thoughtful gestures. Sharing food that you've made during us-time is an important kind of thoughtful gesture which can be given and then appreciated. We love this diary entry that Sam made to tell us about the ritual around preparing Marmite on toast for herself and her partner, Alex.

Explaining this drawing, Sam says:

'I get up and go to the shop for the newspaper leaving Alex reading her book in bed. I come back and make her tea, me coffee, and marmite on toast. I have a strange habit of always giving the best or most perfect toast to her – I always take the worst of whatever it is for myself. Alex must always have the best as she deserves it. If one bit of toast is a bit burnt or inferior to the other one in some way then that must be mine.'

For Sam and Alex food says more than a thousand words ever could. Through her gift of Marmite on toast, Sam demonstrates how much her partner means to her. No one else would be able to read the meaning of this gift, and that's the point. Through this gesture Sam and Alex speak to each other in their own language of love.

So us-time has many functions in our relationships. It's a time to give and receive thoughtful gestures, gifts, appreciation, and compliments. It demonstrates that we're invested in

29

each other and provides an opportunity for nurturing our relationship. It also gives us the opportunity to engage in shared interests, to communicate, to be physically close, and to create the kinds of memories which bond us together over time.

We'll return to many of these themes again through the rest of the book. For now it's important to touch on balancing together-time with time-apart.

Together and separate: us-time and me-time

You might think it's odd to list 'me-time' as something that people do to sustain their relationships. However, most people agree that it's vital to have some time apart.

One reason for this is that having separate time gives us a sense of independence and a way of maintaining our own identities. Many people find that they lose their sense of themselves a bit in relationships, or that they start to feel like they can't make their own choices any more. At worst this can mean that a relationship begins to feel suffocating or overwhelming.

'I like most that we can do our own things without hassle.'

'We're not in each other's pockets.'

In terms of what people actually do in their time apart, it's often important that it's something that's separate from both family and work. The most common examples include hobbies, personal interests, and individual friendships. For some it's just about taking time out. For example, Kaylee said:

'Being alone is something I love. I find a lot of peace when I'm in silence. I find I'm able to rest and to be with myself. I'm able to think. As much as I'm active and like to explore the outside, I also like to be still. It's something I need and I always try to make sure I get some of it during the week.'

Before we get into this more, think about whether you have any time in your life that you spend alone without a partner, friend or work. If you do, what does this time mean to you? If not, is it something you'd like? Or you might find the idea difficult, perhaps see it as unnecessary or even self-indulgent? We're going to explore some of these points now.

Looking after number one

People often struggle with the idea of taking me-time because they see it as selfish in some way. The messages we get about relationships often tell us that we should spend all of our time together. Love-song lyrics talk of being with each other always, or everywhere, or never being apart. In reality this can make it difficult when we'd actually prefer some space in our relationship. People often assume, for example, that there's something wrong if partners ask for 'time out', or if they like to take different holidays, do things apart at weekends, go to bed at different times, or sleep separately (we'll return to this in Chapter 4).

As you'll see in Chapter 6, most people said that the most important person in their lives was their partner or their child. However around one in ten people said that – actually – the most important person in their life was themselves.

These people generally didn't give what you might think of as 'selfish' reasons for valuing themselves so highly. In fact they felt that looking after number one was a vital foundation for their relationships. In order to meet the needs and expectations of their partners – and others in their lives – they needed a certain sense of security and stability in themselves.

'Because if I can't look after myself, I can't look after anyone else.'

'My partner has greater needs than I do and our relationship feels more focused on meeting those, so I feel I need to look after myself so I'm able to be there for her.'

Time alone can help you to stay confident in your personal abilities. In relationships it can become easy to let somebody else do certain tasks like driving, cooking, DIY or making phone calls. Time alone means that you have to invest in those skills, and perhaps you're therefore more independent and less anxious about what might happen if your partner wasn't around.

Me-time also enables us to express different sides of ourselves, the sides that come out with friends or when pursuing different interests, for example. This can help to keep a relationship fresh rather than us feeling limited to being only half of a couple: the side of ourselves that we are with that particular person.

Finally, going back to everyday kindness, it can be difficult to be kind to others if we're not able to be kind to ourselves. Many of us find that alone time is an important way of doing some self-care and personal reflection, which – in turn – can leave us more appreciative of our partner, more able to be kind towards them, and less prone to being argumentative. For example, Kaylee said:

'You do need time away, not large amounts of time, but time to do your own things as well as doing things together.'

Do any of these reasons for me-time particularly resonate with you? Do you think it can be a foundation for time with a partner, or a way of keeping up your independence or individual skills, or something to keep a relationship fresh or kind?

Negotiating me-time

Perhaps because of the emphasis in our culture on partners spending all their time together, many people say that it can be difficult to negotiate time apart in their relationships. You may well have found this too. It's another area where people can have quite very different preferences. Often one partner feels the need for more personal space than the other.

'Sometimes I want to be alone and he wants togetherness.'

It's particularly difficult for people who're keen for some us-time in their relationship, due to their busy hectic lives, to appreciate that they also need to make space for me-time in the small amount of time that they have available.

Another difficulty here is the 'relationship escalator', something we'll return to in Chapter 6. This is the common idea in our culture that, over time, relationships should become closer and closer. Any move away from closeness and towards greater distance is seen as a bad sign or even an indicator of an impending break-up. You can only go up the escalator because it only moves in that direction.

Ria captures well how difficult the relationship escalator makes it for her to negotiate time apart from her partner. It's testimony to the strength of their relationship that this couple found a safe way to listen to each other and to accommodate their individual needs.

'It's not easy to tell the person that you love that you want to spend more time away from them, and that when they get closer to you, you feel like punching them in the face! It was really hard and it must have been really hard for her to swallow but she dealt with it so well. I mean she was angry for about five minutes and then after that she just said, "Well, if that's what you need, that's what you need and that's what we'll do." '

Many people find that, in the reality of their relationship, the escalator actually moves in both directions. Sometimes it feels right to spend more time together; sometimes you need to have a bit more separateness. Flexibility about this is important.

To give a simple example, Anne and Henry discussed how Anne's change of diet had altered their mealtimes. Early on in their relationship, cooking was something that Henry had done for Anne: it was part of his language of love:

Henry: I always used to cook for us, but now you're vegetarian we cook separate meals.

Anne: Yes, people seem to think it's really strange. Like my driving instructor, he always laughed about it, 'oh you guys cook separately'. He found it quite amusing, but I don't know.

Henry: Sometimes we have—

Anne: —we have pudding together!

Henry and Anne also talked about the ways in which being on different timetables had changed their eating habits. The combination of factors means that their us-time now revolves around different things than cooking and eating.

The response of Anne's driving instructor shows how difficult it can be if other people think that we're trying to move down the relationship escalator. Comments from people outside the relationship can make it hard for us when we go against the grain, contravening expectations about what 'couples are supposed to do together'.

People prefer both us-time and me-time to be things that they've personally chosen or negotiated between them, rather than things they feel forced into, either by social expectations or by their partner's preferences. This explains why time apart featured highly on the lists of what women in our study liked both best *and* least about their relationships!

Try drawing this kind of diagram – alone or with your partner – to consider the areas of your lives that you like to share and the ones that you like to keep separate. Perhaps first draw it as how things stand at the moment, and then consider any changes you'd like to make to meet your different needs for togetherness and separateness. Importantly, there's no

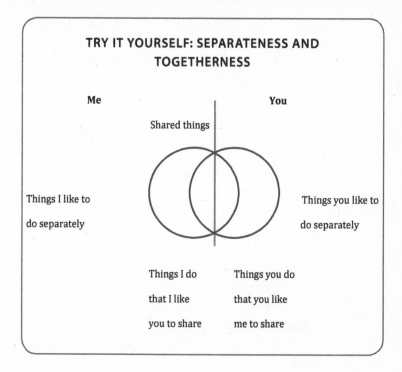

TRY IT YOURSELF: SEPARATENESS AND TOGETHERNESS

Me · You

Shared things

Things I like to do separately

Things you like to do separately

Things I do that I like you to share

Things you do that you like me to share

'right' or 'wrong' amount of sharedness or aloneness; rather different things work for different people and relationships, and at different times in your life.

The tension between separateness and togetherness isn't an easy one to navigate. In fact, many philosophers have spent their lives writing weighty tomes about how hard this is, which is worth remembering when you're struggling with it! Josh and Brendan nicely sum up the inevitability of these kinds of tensions.

Josh: I think just the fact that people are different means you'll never, ever find someone that's exactly the same as you in every respect. There'll always be things which one of you prefers more than the other, doesn't like and the other does, or likes done in a certain way.

Brendan: I think along with that everyone has got different expectations of what's nice, what's normal, what's going over the top.

We'll return to this theme in the next chapter when we think about how people navigate shared and separate space in their homes, and in Chapter 5 when we explore the separate activities and relationships that people value.

Conclusions

Relationship advice often talks a lot about doing 'relationship work'. Hopefully this chapter has shown you that people certainly *do* work to nurture and sustain their relationships. But this work often involves the very ordinary, everyday stuff that people do all the time, rather than big conversations or life changes.

These kinds of things are also a kind of preventative measure for the tougher times that inevitably come in any relationship. For Debs, thoughtful gestures, words of appreciation, us-time and me-time are all like an investment she and her partner are making in the bank account of their relationship:

'What makes our relationship work is that it's like a bank account. We go through periods when we're having a hard time, usually because of external stuff, rather than fundamental problems in the relationship: We're just not getting enough sleep or one of the kids is being really horrible or something. But, because our relationship feels so strong, and we've been making deposits in it for so long, that's okay and we can keep going. It feels like we're withdrawing from the relationship, but it's alright because it doesn't run out of money.'

SUMMARY SUGGESTIONS: EVERYDAY KINDNESS

Here are a few more things to try yourself, based on this chapter. If you're not currently in a partner relationship these things work great with friends and family as well. Just make sure you check with the other person that these things will be appreciated before trying them!

- Surprise them with a random act of kindness, perhaps a meal at the end of the day, a Post-it love note, or text message letting them know you're thinking of them. Or bring them their favourite drink in bed, whether that's a cup of tea or a cocktail!
- Show gratitude for something they regularly do for you and that you've stopped saying 'thank you' for. Try doing this every day for a week.
- Make space for some us-time over the next week: maybe a movie you want to watch together, or sharing each other's favourite activities or cooking with each other.
- Make time for yourself sometime over the next week: perhaps an hour in a cafe, a walk in the park or window shopping, or catching up with a friend.

CHAPTER 2

ON THE HOME FRONT

The ache for home lives in all of us, the safe place where we
can go as we are and not be questioned.

– Maya Angelou

I n the last chapter it might've struck you how much of the important everyday business of relationships happens in the home. People bring each other cups of tea, thank each other for doing the chores, or cuddle up on the sofa to watch TV. They appreciate starting the morning together, or coming

Feet up, cup of tea,
Will be home with my
girl very soon.

x x x   x x x

home to each other after a day at work. One person gave us this picture to show a good moment in their relationship.

In fact, this focus on home might *not* have struck you because it's so integral to many relationships. The role of home in our relationships can be like water for fishes: we don't notice it's there but we wouldn't stay alive without it! As we've already seen it's often helpful to turn our attention to these things we usually take for granted. Also, not all relationships take place within a shared home, and many people these days have a more complex relationship to where they live. So let's think some more about home.

You've seen in the last chapter that many people find that both time apart and time together are important in their relationships. These can be hard to negotiate when you don't share the same living space, and also when you do.

QUIZ TIME: SHARED OR SEPARATE SPACE AND TIME?

Before we go on, delve a little deeper into your own feelings on sharing time and space. You can fill this in for a current, past, or imagined future partner. Just circle the answer that's closest to your own preference.

1. You and your partner are travelling away separately this weekend, to see old friends. How much contact would you like with them while you're apart?
(a) I'd prefer that we both only go away for one day of the weekend so that we don't have a night apart.
(b) I'd like my partner to check in with texts or a phone call before bedtime each day we're apart.
(c) I'm happy with no contact while we're apart, and I'll use the time to do my own stuff, like see my friends.

2. How important is it to you to schedule regular time with your partner?
(a) We don't need to schedule it because we spend most evenings and weekends together anyway.

(b) We try to book in at least one 'date night' a week to definitely spend time together.

(c) The idea of having to schedule time feels too rigid; I'd prefer that we just go with the flow and see each other when we want to.

3. Which would be your preferred living situation?

(a) Living together as a couple, or as a family if we have any children.

(b) I'd like to live together but I'm open to different possibilities, like living in a shared house or living apart some of the time if one of us worked away from home.

(c) I'd rather live separately or in a situation where we had plenty of space from each other.

4. What would be your ideal scenario for managing domestic finances?

(a) We'd have a joint account and pool our income.

(b) We'd negotiate it. Maybe one of us would pay a greater share of the bills if we earned a lot more than the other.

(c) I'd rather keep all money separate, with each of us paying an equal share of the housing costs and bills.

5. If you share a house, how do you feel about rooms?

(a) I'd rather it was all 'our space'; we'd mostly be in the same room together when we're at home anyway.

(b) It'd be good if we both had somewhere that was more our own personal space, like the kitchen for one person and the garden for the other.

(c) I would only consider living with someone if we had our own separate rooms.

6. How much do you want to know about your partner's life?

(a) I'd expect them to tell me everything and vice versa, to the extent that we'd look at each other's phone messages, emails or social media, for example.

(b) I don't need to know every thought in their head, but I wouldn't want any secrets.

(c) I definitely need to have privacy: areas of my life that I don't share with them.

7. Is it important to you to spend leisure time together?

(a) Yes. I'd expect us to spend most of our free time doing things we enjoy together.

(b) Probably there'd be a couple of hobbies or interests that we didn't share, but we'd do most stuff together.

(c) Not that important. I have other people I like to do stuff with too.

How did you score?

Mostly a: You like a lot of togetherness and shared time in your relationship. You see yourself very much as a unit and you don't feel the need for a lot of privacy or personal space. You may feel quite insecure if your partner isn't around or checking in with you regularly.

Mostly b: You seem to prefer a balance. While your relationship is important to you, you also like to keep some independence and other things in your life. You might find that sometimes you want a bit more closeness, but other times you'd like a bit more space.

Mostly c: It's important for you to keep a strong sense of yourself as a separate person in your relationships. You maintain your own interests, friends, and space, and you can feel trapped and constrained if you share too much.

You might well find that you gave quite different answers (As, Bs and Cs) to different questions. We often have different preferences about separateness and togetherness in different areas of our lives. For example you might be happy sharing finances but want to keep some parts of your life private, or it might be important to do things together but you don't need to live together. Hopefully this quiz helped you to see where you are on a separate–together spectrum.

Separate   Together

Remember, there are no 'rights' or 'wrongs' here. Different people in a relationship may well be in different places from each other on this spectrum, depending on who they are, their backgrounds, and the other things that are going on in their lives. Our place on this spectrum is also likely to change over time. Recognising and respecting that you and a partner may have different preferences is vital when navigating any differences. Things may become tricky if one of you is sure that you have the 'right' way of doing things as you'll see when we explore conflict in the next chapter.

Now let's look at how different people manage their relationships whether they live apart or together, and the role that our homes have in enduring love.

Living apart together

Over the last few years there's been a lot of media coverage of people who 'live apart together': LAT relationships. This isn't really a new phenomenon though. Some partners have always chosen to live separately, some or all of the time.

Living apart might happen through choice, as with wealthy couples who have two homes, for example. Alternatively it might be because circumstances demand it, such as when one partner works away from home in the military services, on an oil rig, or overseas. Many people find they have to live apart for work reasons in a difficult economic climate.

LAT relationships seem to be on the increase with around four million people in the UK currently living separately from a partner. We didn't focus specifically on LATs in our study, but we did find that over one in ten people were in that kind of living situation.

VITAL STATISTICS:

Living Situations

This is how the people in our survey broke down in terms of their type of relationship and living situation.
- 63% married or civil partnership and living together
- 24% living together but not married/civilly partnered
- 11% living apart together
- 2% going out together

At the same time that we were doing our study, another group of researchers – Simon Duncan, Sasha Roseneil and Miranda Phillips – were studying LAT relationships in the UK in a lot more detail. They found that people gave a whole array of different reasons for not cohabiting.

Choosing to live apart

For people who see living apart together as a choice, some are initially forced to live separately by circumstances but come to embrace it and to see the positive side. Others see it as more of a deliberate choice, perhaps as a better way of living for them or as a way of staying more independent. As author Angela Neustatter puts it, many LAT couples are:

'Deeply committed to each other, but... know themselves well enough to be wary of blending their lives too thoroughly, aware they need separateness to be able to retreat entirely from the presence, requirements, demands, delights, of a partner who is not less loved because of this.'

Other reasons that people choose to live apart are perhaps less positive. As you saw in the last chapter, research shows that domestic chores are still unequally shared in relationships between women and men. Simon Duncan and his colleagues found that women in relationships with men are particularly likely to choose to live apart so that they can avoid these kinds of inequalities.

In our study Ayesha and Jack spoke about the pros and cons of living apart versus living together, and how their decision was driven by practicalities as much as preferences. Ayesha said that living apart would really be her ideal scenario. This came as something of a surprise to Jack!

Ayesha: Living as a couple is so much cheaper than living separately. I've always wanted to live on my own, that would be a dream but I've never been able to afford it.

Jack: Really it's your dream to live on your own?

Ayesha: Just have some Zen place where I can do a lot of reflection.

Jack: See I like living with Ayesha. This is the limit for me!

Ayesha: Ah see I like living with you and I enjoy that, but I also liked it when we didn't live together and we had our separate spaces.

Jack: Yes I agree to a degree.

Ayesha: I think having space is important. But at the moment it's very difficult to buy a house if you're a single person, you need two incomes to afford a mortgage.

Jack: Or very generous parents or something.

Take a moment to think about whether you relate more to Ayesha or Jack in this exchange. We'll come back to your own views on living apart together soon.

Being forced to live apart

Unlike Ayesha, many of the LATs we spoke to didn't *want* to live apart. In fact, they often listed it as one of the top things they disliked about their relationships.

'For financial reasons we both live with our respective families, which means it can be difficult to be on our own to talk, cuddle and relax with each other.'

'We don't live together due to financial and logistical circumstances so we don't spend enough time together.'

There are many reasons why people are prevented from living together, such as geographical or economic circumstances like visa restrictions or work opportunities. People in these kinds of long-distance relationship generally regret them and hope that they'll be able to change this situation in the future.

Some people have to live apart because families or communities won't accept their relationship. This might be because their families aren't accepting of same-sex relationships or because the relationship is with someone from a different faith or culture. Sometimes people live apart because one person is already married to somebody else and feels unable or unwilling to separate from them. In these situations there's often a strong desire to set up home together and a great sense of sadness that it isn't possible.

In our research, and in the LAT study, partners often saw living apart as a temporary phase rather than a long-term scenario. The relationship escalator that we talked about in the last chapter generally sees moving in together as an inevitable stage in a relationship after people have been together for some period of time. Living apart can be misread by other people as a sign of relationship problems or a lack of commitment. It can be difficult for long-term LATs to resist these pressures because other people often question them about when they're moving in together, or why they live apart.

Think about whether there are situations in your own life which might make living apart from a partner necessary. How would – or do – you feel about this? Do you generally see living apart as a temporary stage in a relationship or something that could be for the long term?

How to live apart

For people who live apart some or all of the time, reunions become really important. They cherish returning home to each other, and remember these times fondly afterwards. They also invest a lot of time and energy in maintaining closeness while they're away, staying in touch online or over the phone. This is something we'll explore more in the next chapter on communication.

There are no rights and wrongs when it comes to living arrangements. LATs speak about many of the same positive aspects and pressures in their relationships as those who live together, and there are some specific pros and cons that come with living apart.

Living separately reduces some of the tensions that happen when you're around each other 24/7. It also seems to help people to avoid falling into conventional gender roles around domestic chores. But there are also different problems that have to be faced, such as the difficulty of arranging time together and the cost of maintaining two separate homes.

Think some more about where you stand on living apart or living together. What's your ideal living situation in a relationship? What living situations would be deal-breakers for you? Would you expect living arrangements to change over the course of a relationship or to stay the same?

If you did – or do – live apart, it can be useful to consider the kinds of relationship practices that we covered in the last chapter. How might those be different? How do you ensure some every-day kindness and connection happens even when you're apart? We'll make some suggestions about this in the next chapter.

Living together apart

So one difficulty for people who live apart is how to get 'us-time'. On the flip side, a major challenge for those who live together is how to get 'me-time'. We saw in the last chapter that both of these things are important and that people often find it difficult to navigate the tension between separateness and togetherness. People who live together have various ways of dividing up their physical space to get some time apart, and they also struggle when they have different preferences about personal space.

If you live with a partner – or have done so in the past – think about whether you've had any separate space or time in the home, and whether you figured that out between you or whether it's happened more spontaneously.

Separate spaces

Some people are able to have different rooms which they can retreat to when they want some space. This might mean a sepa-rate bedroom for each person, both having a study area, or one person having a room in the house and the other having a garden shed or garage workshop, for example. People negotiate different rules about such spaces, including whether the other person can go into it when they aren't around, or whether they should knock on the door before entering if their partner is in there.

Of course separate rooms for each partner, or for all members of a family, just isn't possible for all of us. People who value having separate spaces often come up with inventive ways of ensuring that they get it. We've spoken with people who've blanketed off an area of a living room or turned a cupboard under the stairs into a meditation chamber. Others very deliberately use going for a bath or out into the garden as a signal that they need time to themselves. Some use spaces outside the home like a pub, park, library, or local cafe.

Darren and Daniela talked about the way Daniela cooks to make sure that the kitchen is seen as her territory. It took them a little longer to figure out where Darren got his personal space!

Darren: When she does the cooking she's in a world of her own. She's just listening to music and stuff like that. At least you're happy, aren't you?

Daniela: Yes that's definitely my area. In the sitting room you can't really control much, because you've got all the kids' toys. And we're all in the bedroom. It's the one area where things are where I want them to be. So yes I probably am a bit of a control freak when it comes to the kitchen! You have to have a space don't you?

Darren: Mine's probably the toilet! No, I suppose mine's the balcony. Sometimes in the evening I'll have a quick cigarette out there. I'll sit there and I'll just mull things over, and then I'm back in and I'm back to normal.

Daniela: That's your corner there in the evening, isn't it?

TOP TIP

If you share a home with other people, and you haven't done it already, create a space that's yours. Figure out what kind of space would work for you and your situation: A separate room? A divided off part of a room? A place that is 'yours' for certain parts of the day? An out-building or garden space? Or a place outside the home you can go to? Think about how you can chat with the people you live with about this space. How will you signal to others when you want to be alone there? The next chapter will help with communicating these kinds of needs.

Navigating tensions

Personal space is often a point of tension between partners because they don't always want the same things at the same times. Garry and Lucy, and Linda and James, used furniture in different ways to ensure more, or less, contact between them. But they all found it difficult to reach an arrangement that met everybody's needs.

Lucy: We quite like our own space and I think some of that comes from the fact that we both lived on our own for quite a significant period of time before being in this relationship. I probably crave more hugging-type affection than you do, would you say that's true?

Garry: Yes.

Lucy: But I've got used to not getting it. You've adopted that sofa, haven't you, over there?

Garry: We gravitate to different positions but it's not by design is it? Although when there's been a swap over very occasionally, the remark will be made, 'don't get too comfortable on my sofa!'

Lucy: All very tongue in cheek.

Linda: James will always sit on the sofa. If I'm on the sofa, he'll always want to sit beside me.

James: Right up against you.

Linda: Yes, in my personal space. I'm not allowed any of that!

James: You get plenty of time too.

Linda: I get plenty of time when you're at work!

Think about whether any of the furniture in your home is 'yours'. How do you feel when other people use it? Are there times when, like Linda, you don't feel that you're allowed personal space? Or, like James, do you find that you're sometimes asking for contact that the other person isn't so keen to give? How does it feel to be on each side of that dynamic?

Work time, home time

Like James and Linda, many people see work as a time when they can legitimately get time apart. For some people this is enough space away from each other and they really cherish the moment of coming back together at the end of the day. For others, work doesn't really feel like proper time to themselves and they need some alone time at home as well.

Also many people work from home at least some of the time. This is a point of tension for partners when one person wants to spend time together and the other needs a separate space to work in. For example, in her diary Fiona said, about her partner:

'Unfortunately she still had work to do on the computer so we spent the evening in different rooms, and we had spent the whole day either apart or with someone else. I don't feel like we have enough time together. Sometimes she can be so wrapped up in computer stuff that I feel like she forgets I'm in the flat at all.'

People can have very different boundaries between work and home. Some like them to be quite fuzzy and want to check emails in the evening or bring work projects home, for example. Others like a much clearer dividing line. It can be tough when partners have different preferences. As Richard says in his diary, managing the boundaries of home life and work life is tricky.

'Back home my partner has cooked. We chat over dinner in the dining room. After I need to work on the computer upstairs for a chunk of the evening. This is probably our biggest area of friction. I know she doesn't like being left alone while I work on the computer but there's a lot for me to keep up with. She leaves me to it while she watches TV downstairs. At some point she calls up to ask if I want a cup of tea, and tempts me beyond endurance with chocolate biscuits. Sometimes she'll call that there's something interesting on the TV.'

Do you relate more to Richard's partner and Fiona in wanting more together-time? Or do you relate more to Fiona's partner and Richard in appreciating time apart, to focus on work?

Again there isn't a right and a wrong way of doing things here. Instead it's about respecting differences and trying to see whether some kind of compromise is possible. It can also be useful to find out what the situation *means* for each person involved.

Perhaps for Richard and for Fiona's partner it's a matter of feeling that work is the first priority in the evening. They want to get it out of the way before they can relax. Or perhaps it's actually a way for them to get some alone-time. For Richard's partner and for Fiona, however, there's a sense that they feel forgotten or rejected because their partner is working in the time that they thought they'd be spending together.

Think about what work means to you. How do you feel about bringing work home with you, or not? Does your partner share those views, or do they see things differently? What are the pros and cons, for you, of a clear dividing line between work and home?

In situations like these, it's worth thinking about whether there are ways of getting both sets of needs met. Can the one partner get the space and time they need for work, and the other partner receive reassurance and some time when they're included? Obviously communication is crucial here, and we'll say a lot more about that in the next chapter.

Separate and together

Zak and his partner were a good example of the kind of negotiation we're talking about here. Zak's a gamer and spends a lot of time playing online. This could have been a source of tension between them, but they found a way to share space that worked for them. They put two screens side-by-side on a desk. Zak proudly showed us how they'd set it up.

'Sometimes I play a video game on there while she's watching a DVD on the other one. We're reminded of how much we enjoy ourselves as individuals. Those periods are very special, very important.'

Interestingly, for Zak and his partner, doing something separately seemed to bond them even closer together. The same can be true for partners who have quite separate lives but feel very connected when they come home and talk over the minutiae of their day. So it is possible for greater separateness to lead to an enhanced sense of togetherness rather than the opposite.

You've seen that there are many possibilities for balancing time apart and time together in the home. These include having separate spaces to retreat to, sharing certain activities but not others, having specific times when you're together and apart, and doing things separately alongside each other to achieve a sense of togetherness and separateness at the same time.

Of course preferences shift and change over time as well. For example, a friend told us that she used to love it when her partner came and chatted with her when she was in the bath... until they had kids. After that, bath-time became something that allowed her to get some space away from everybody else. For other people, preferences about sleeping together or holidaying together change in response to changes in work situations, retirement, or physical illness.

As we said in the last chapter, there's no easy answer to the tensions around separateness and togetherness. Different people negotiate it in different ways. It's useful to see how people who live together find separate spaces and opportunities for alone time, *and* how people in LAT relationships work to build in closeness and time together.

Think some more about your own needs for space and time apart, and for company and time together.

- Where have the separate/together tensions occurred in your relationships?
- What versions of me-time and us-time work for you?
- How have you negotiated time and space together and apart?
- How have these things changed over time?

If this is still a tricky area for you it's worth noting down your preferences for now, and we'll talk about how you can communicate about any differences in the next chapter.

Ideal homes?

A lot of people told us about their 'ideal' homes, either the ways in which they wanted to change the homes they already lived in, or the kind of home they'd like to have some day, if they could afford it.

People often imagined their ideal homes as the ones that would enable them to live their relationships in exactly the ways they wanted to, instead of feeling constrained by the space around them. The kind of homes they wanted were also often shaped by their experiences growing up.

Before reading on, think a bit about your own ideal home – or even sketch out what it might look like. How would you design it to fit your own relationship or the relationship that you'd like to have in the future?

The perfect home, the perfect relationship?

As you've seen, people who don't already live together place a lot of importance on getting their own home. For some this means buying a property. For others rented space feels fine – so long as they can make it their own with furniture and decorations. For example, Eleri and Alun talked about how the small, rather cramped, apartment that they now rent is really special to them.

> **Eleri:** It's ours.
> **Alun:** It's our space.
> **Eleri:** It's not even ours, we rent it.
> **Alun:** Yes, it's rented! But it's our home.
> **Eleri:** It's ours and it's the first one we've had together.
> **Alun:** Yes, it's the first place we've had together and we've made it very much our own and we like it.

When people imagine their ideal homes it's not so much about ownership but about having a space that allows them to be together and separate in just the ways they want to be. For example, several people said that a sense of space was important.

> *'I want a home that feels spacious enough. This space isn't suited to us. It's three rooms that we have to do everything in. We can't have a meal together.'*

> *'At the moment because we're tidying up we're mostly in the same rooms, but we're planning to split and have two sitting rooms: one for the kids and one for us.'*

Louise and Luke described changes to their house they'd like to make so that they could have the specific kind of togetherness which they enjoyed. This was partly driven by Luke's childhood memories of his family home.

> **Luke:** Kitchens for me are always the heart of the house. I grew up in a house with a really lovely big kitchen which was where everyone just hung out.
> **Louise:** If the flat was ours and we were allowed to we'd take this wall out and have an open-plan space so you could be in the living room talking to the person who's cooking. You just can't do that now. Our flat's very functional but it's not particularly conducive to collaboration.

Others wanted space to give them the possibility of spending time apart. For example, Kris said that being employed would allow him and Noel to get a place where they weren't 'under each other's feet' all the time. He talked about his own dream home:

'It would be nothing flash or extravagant, just something with a bit of space, so that if one of the kids wants to go to her room she can go there without the other one following her.'

Other people wanted more space so that they could more easily invite friends and family into their home. Emma and Jack said that if they didn't have neighbours above and below them they wouldn't be so concerned about noise; friends could come and relax with them, in their space, staying the night if they needed to. Jack said that their previous home was even worse for socialising:

'In our previous flat the only place they could sleep was the living room. And because it was a converted house, to get from the bedroom to the bathroom you had to walk through the living room, which just wasn't on!'

Do you connect with any of these ideal home ideas particularly: the desire to have enough space, to be able to communicate easily with people in other rooms, to have separate space for each person, or to be able to socialise and have people stay over?

Several people talked about the future possibilities that would open up if they had the kind of home they wanted. They spoke about things like setting aside a room and decorating it in a particular way for a child, or having an outside space for growing food. The idea of having an 'outside room' – a garden space that's part of the home – was a common feature, often linked to a sense that it'd help relationships flourish too.

Many people want a home that will be 'theirs' for the rest of their lives. For Anna that means a place big enough to have children in, and with enough privacy to accommodate the kind of sexual relationship that she and her partner enjoy.

'I want to live in my house for about 30, 40 years. I don't want to sell and move again! If we're ever going to have children, we're going to have to have at least a three-bedroomed house, because it gives us the space to grow.

'Our house is going to be somewhere that reflects us, that we can use as we want to. Our sexual activities are very restricted by this house because we can't put any solid anchor points in without someone else asking, "What's that there? Why's that there?"

'It's that opportunity to be able to tailor the house to us – to what we want to do with it and how we want to conduct our lives in it – so that it becomes our space and not just the place we happen to live in.'

Making a home *'our space and not just the place we happen to live in'* can be done through furniture, fixtures and fittings, but in other instances – as Anna says – it's about putting down roots and taking up residency. The main restriction on this is often financial. For example, one couple had to put their house in one of their parents' names due to money problems, which meant that it didn't feel like it really belonged to them. For another couple, taking in a lodger helped to pay the bills but meant that they didn't always have the house to themselves, and so they couldn't plan time together in the way they'd like.

Which aspects of home that we've covered here are most important for you? Does owning a place play a vital role in how you imagine your ideal future together? If this isn't possible, how are you creating a sense of permanency now and into the future? Is it important to have enough space to enable time together and/or time apart? What about having enough space for friends and family to visit? Or having somewhere that you can extend, in the future, to accommodate a family, to grow things, or to develop new interests?

You've seen that homes can be very important for partners' everyday practices: they can help to build fond memories together, and to build imagined futures together. Home can symbolise security, commitment and connectedness in a relationship. We'll now explore these meanings of home in a bit more detail.

The meanings of home

In her book, *A Home for the Heart*, Angela Neustatter considers the different meanings of home for relationships. She also explores various experiments in doing home differently such as cohousing projects and other shared living and childcare arrangements.

As in our study, she found that different things work for different people, and at different times in their relationships. She suggests that we need to move away from a one-size-fits-all understanding of homes, to embrace the diversity of possibilities. This might also help us to address the various economic, social, and emotional pressures that face us at the moment.

Many people who Angela Neustatter interviewed said that home was the place where they could be their 'private, authentic selves'. Wafting from empty room to empty room, 'veging out' in front of the TV in their pants, or dancing in the bedroom – people can let loose at home and be free from worries about what anybody else thinks of them.

The philosopher Alain de Botton says that the daily rituals of home (washing, cooking, eating, sleeping, tending plants, looking after pets etc.) also connect us in a fundamental way to the rest of humanity – who are all doing the same things.

So home can be both something that frees us *and* something that connects us. You might feel connected, reading this chapter, to some of the everyday home activities that people have mentioned that are also familiar to you.

Freedom and connection also come into how we create our homes. However big or small the space, we often fashion it to make it ours, using objects, pictures, and music, as a kind of extension of ourselves. Alain de Botton calls homes the 'guardians of identity' for this reason. But, as we've seen in this chapter, we also create homes together, with other people, making joint decisions about furniture or paint colours and investing time and energy in creating a place that reflects our relationship, family, or group of housemates.

Think about the ways in which home is a place of freedom for you, and the ways in which it's a place of connection. When you think about home you might think more about privacy, independence and being yourself, or you might think more about feeling safe, grounded, and a sense of belonging. Or it might be a bit of both.

So home is something that can represent our freedom and it's something that can express our connection with others as part of something larger. The people who spoke to Angela Neustatter about their homes often said that they were the place where they *belonged*. Home was where they felt their strongest. They've built up a physical and emotional collection of stories in their home with others and alone, in good times and in bad.

One woman in our study, Debs, beautifully illustrates this. Her relationship story was totally embedded in the bricks and mortar of the home that she and her partner shared.

'We're both quite homey. It's far more than a place to lay your head. And we love this house. We moved here and within two weeks I was pregnant which felt very psychologically signifi-cant. I felt so 'at home' that I was able to get pregnant! And then I lost that baby, so it's not quite such a nice story, but it's part of our story about how right this place feels to us and how impor-tant it is to us to live here. Not just in the house but in the wider community. We both feel very settled, and that's important.'

Home gave Debs a safety net that held her through some hugely difficult times. This reminds us that our ideal home might not be picture perfect, like the chocolate box house with roses around the front door. Instead it's more about being a place of sanctuary: a repository for trials and tribulations, hearts and heartache.

It's important to point out that home certainly isn't a positive place for everyone. We've seen that it's important for home to be a place where we can feel grounded and expand our imaginations. In situations of poverty, social marginalisation, homelessness and overcrowding, homes may not be secure enough for this. And when our homes involve physical or emotional danger, we're deprived of the peace and privacy that we need to feel safe, or to feel free.

There are other times when homes stop being nurturing. For some people, the pressure to have the perfect home, like the pressure to have a perfect relationship, can keep them boxed up in very unhappy homes, or constantly moving on in search of something better. Home can also become suffocating – a cage we've trapped ourselves in – rather than a valuable shelter that we can retreat into and come out stronger. People might cling too tightly to an ideal of home rather than recognising that we can find moments of being 'at home' with many people and in many places.

Ask yourself, and any people you live with: what does home mean to you? What were your experiences of home growing up? To what extent has this shaped what you think of as home today? Can you describe your most positive and negative experiences of home? These questions can help you to think some more about what you're looking for from a home.

Partners will never agree on everything, but if we can understand what home means to each person, we'll be better prepared for the business of building and sharing a home together, if that's something that we decide to do.

Home comforts

In our research we used something called emotion maps to study people's home lives in detail. We drew a rough floor plan of people's houses or flats with them and then, for a week, they put stickers on these maps to show us how their relationship happened in these spaces, and whereabouts in their homes people had different emotions. It became clear that certain areas were *comfort zones* where partners shared happy or contented times. Other areas were *hot spots* where arguments and conflicts often bubbled up.

TRY IT YOURSELF: EMOTION MAPS

To try an emotion map yourself you'll need a large sheet of paper and some coloured stickers (which you can get from most stationery shops). If you don't want to buy stickers, you can just draw on faces with different emotions using different coloured pens.

To begin with, go around your home and sketch out a floor plan. This forms the basis of your emotion map. It doesn't have to be exact or detailed, just a sense of which rooms are where. If you have multiple floors then you can draw these separately alongside each other. It's up to you whether you include any outside areas, or vehicles, sheds, etc. in the plan. For example, a plan might look something like this (it's fine either to draw it freehand, or to do it on a computer like we've done here):

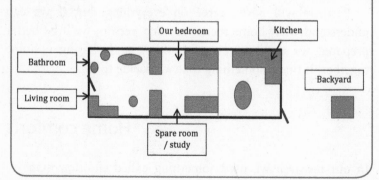

Then, decide which colour sticker you're going to use for each person. Use different colours for the different people you want to represent, including yourself and any partners, family, friends, pets, and so on. You'll probably want to create stickers for anyone who fairly regularly spends time in your home.

Draw different emoticons on the different colours (some of each emotion on each colour). We used the following emoticons to represent each of these emotions. But you can always add further ones as well. You can also stick two together when you want to represent mixed feelings.

For the next week put the stickers onto your map each time you and other people in your home feel or express an emotion. You can complete it over the course of the day as and when you have time, or at the end of each day, thinking back to what's happened and where. It's fine to give a general sense of where feelings happen rather than remembering exact events. You could also note rough timings if you'd like to think about *when* as well as *where* emotions tend to happen (e.g., first thing in the morning, after a meal, or when you're heading into or out of the house).

At the end of the week take a look at your map. Make a note of what strikes you about it. If you live with a partner you could each make an emotion map and then compare them. Or you could try making one together and chatting at the end of each day about where you want to place the stickers. Really it's up to you how you do it.

Once you've done this, think about whereabouts in the home different interactions happen. Do particular emotions happen with different activities? Are there any patterns that you can see? You could talk through answers to these questions with your partner while looking at your emotion map.

Comfort zones and hot spots

Here's an example of a completed emotion map so you can see what one looks like.

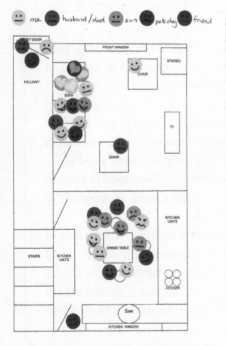

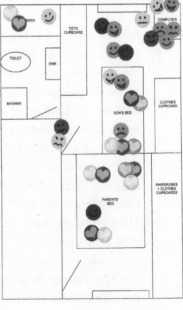

You can see from this map that, as with many people, the sofa was a happy place for this family to be as they cuddled up to watch TV in the evening. They also shared contented times with children and friends in the living room and round the kitchen table. Both the parents' bed and the child's bed were places of love (including much love from the dog when he was allowed up on the bed!).

So beds, sofas, and dining tables are often comfort zones, with just occasional upsets or arguments happening there. However, two major hot spots in this house were around the computer and around doorways. Again lots of other people share these hot spots. Many people fight about partners or children being on the computer when they want to prioritise together time. Computers can also be a source of tension if more than one person wants to use them. In this case the computer was a hot spot because of the mum's concerns that her son was playing games when he should be doing his homework.

Doorways often end up framing arguments, both symbolically and literally! Our colleague Renee Singh uses emotion maps in her counselling work with families. She too found that families often put a lot of angry faces near the door where they enter and exit the house. In one family, the father explained that he found it most difficult to negotiate differences in parenting styles between him and his wife when leaving the house. He often lost his temper because he felt that nobody else was organised enough to be ready on time.

One mother in our research, Joan, put her hot spots in quite different places.

'I found it interesting doing the floor plan because I noticed there were patterns in the rooms, especially in the kitchen. It seemed like quite an unhappy, grumpy place where I was telling the children off around the fridge, around the cooker, and the sink. It starts off quite happy at the table and then we sit down on an evening and by the end…

'The kids must think, 'this is a grumpy area, she's going to tell us off again now, let's wait for it'. They must just think that and try and push it as far as they can get.'

We'll talk about hot spots around chores and children more in the next chapter when we think about how to manage conflicts. For now, remember that emotion maps can identify positive events as well as negative. Doing this activity can help you to notice some of the everyday acts of kindness that we covered in the last chapter that you might otherwise take for granted.

Debs, who we met earlier, used her emotion map to locate points of closeness. She found that the kitchen was definitely 'the heart of the home' where the family ate together and shared much love and contentment. Tenderness with her partner happened in hallways and doorways – where they shared a snatched cuddle as they swapped over childcare 'shifts' or greeted each other coming home from work. These were particularly fond moments for Debs, as was seeing the kid's delight when a parent returned to the house. So, as you can see, doorways may be hot spots for some people and comfort zones for others.

Watching TV together

Many people in our study said that the sofa was one of their main comfort zones because this was where they curled up together at the end of a day to watch TV. We already touched on this in the last chapter but it's worth saying some more about this because the TV series or box set was such an important feature in our research. Several people spoke at length about the importance of *The Wire*, *Orange is the New Black*, or some similar show, in giving them together time.

This simple activity has different meanings for people. For example, some find it's a good time to have some physical closeness.

'It was just a very intimate thing to do; to just sit there and be on the sofa together and watch a TV show. It just felt really nice.'

Other people find that an episode of a series is the perfect length for some quality time together which meets both of their needs. Louise and Luke said that it could be difficult to get such time because Louise is really tired in the evenings while Luke often wants to get chores done or to talk about parenting issues. Watching *The Sopranos* is a good compromise for them both.

> **Louise:** We got a box set that we both like. It does mean we've sat down together for the first time in months and months. We've watched something every other evening and that's been really nice.
>
> **Luke:** Yes it has. It's good it's about the right length of time. Because that's the other thing: I don't mind sitting down to watch something if it doesn't really eat up time or is at the expense of the state of the house. The mob brought us together!
>
> **Louise:** And compared to Tony Soprano he's a really good dad.
>
> **Luke:** Yes, so it's great, we watch that and I go 'look at him!'

You can see for Luke and Louise that the *content* of the series they watch is helpful, as well as the *process* of watching it. Louise can express her appreciation of Luke's fathering in a jokey manner by comparing him to Tony Soprano!

Some people find that the quality of what they watch isn't even that important, it's just watching something together which matters. For example, one couple described downloading a terrible movie. They bonded over how bad they both found it and enjoyed laughing about it again later when they described it to us.

Other people find that playing computer games together has a similar function to watching TV. They can round off a day that way, escaping from things that are bothering them and sharing the experience.

In his diary, Gareth described a day with his partner that started with sharing TV but ended up escalating into a particularly special time for their relationship.

'In the afternoon we watched the end of The West Wing. *We basically drank quite heavily for the rest of the day! It's not that often that we have weekends off together at home, especially when Tony doesn't have any work that needs doing urgently so it was really nice and relaxing. We started watching* Tinker Tailor Soldier Spy *in the evening, but were a bit too drunk to follow it, instead we ended up putting a load of music on and had a little impromptu party instead. It was a really fun day.'*

Think about the role of TV, computer games, or other forms of entertainment in your relationship. Is this something that's important to you and, if so, in what ways? Remember a recent example where you shared some entertainment with somebody close – what made it so enjoyable? Is it about the chance for physical closeness, for example, or more that you're sharing an experience, or having a laugh together?

Like Gareth and Tony, many people say that moments of impromptu silliness are important in their relationships. A particularly common theme here – which surprised us and might surprise you too – was dancing.

Dancing

Several people said that dancing together was an especially enjoyable moment which bonded them together. Like cooking, which we mentioned in the last chapter, dancing is something that people who don't have a lot of time, space or money, can do together anyway.

For Glen it's particularly sweet because the whole family can share it. *'We were all cuddling each other and dancing and it was really funny.'*

Like watching TV, dancing means different things to different people. It can be a spontaneous moment of silliness and frivolity, it can be a more deliberate way of holding the blues at bay, or it can be a moment of sexiness or physical intimacy. For some people it marked the start of their evening, together: passing one earpiece of their headphones to their partner so they can share the end of the song they were listening to on the way home. Others dance together while getting ready in the morning as a way of welcoming the day.

When she explained her emotion map, Sam spoke about how dancing and 'being daft' enabled her and her partner Alex to step out of the heaviness of their lives and into something more light-hearted. They were on welfare benefits and cared for an elderly relative as well as managing mental health problems themselves. Dancing helped them to have a lively moment away from the 'carpet slippers' of coupledom which they found it easy to slip into, having been together for so long.

'We drink wine and watch TV. By the time that the music documentary finishes at 9.55, we are quite tipsy. WE LOVE THIS BAND! WE HAVE ALL THEIR ALBUMS. DANCING MAKES US HAPPY! I put on the HiFi and we both dance to our favourite music. We went to bed very late. It was fun. I always have fun with Alex.'

TOP TIP

If dancing together or sharing music isn't something you've tried, give it a go! Do any of the examples we've given here particularly appeal to you? If so, think about how you could bring them into your own relationships. Creating a mix-CD or online playlist for each other, with music that you share or that makes you think of the other person, can be a great starting point.

Like watching TV series together, dancing and music can become a kind of anchor for a relationship. These things can be something that partners enjoy looking back on together – 'Do you remember when we were watching the *Bake Off* that summer you were pregnant?' Or you might share a wry smile when a certain song comes on the radio, or break into 'your' silly dance.

Conclusions

In a way dancing's a good metaphor for many of the things we've covered in this chapter. Everyone who shares a home does a kind of dance: between together space and separate space, and between the different needs and preferences of the people in the relationship. For example, in her diary Rosemary talked about how, after many years of marriage, she'd learnt a kind of dance with her husband between different rooms and activities.

'After lunch my husband stayed in the front room while I stayed in the back sitting room doing my diary. I took over his seat in the front room as he's NOT very keen on what I watch on TV. We then swapped over rooms so he could watch his TV show.'

Whether living together or living apart, few of us actually live in our ideal homes, and most of us have constraints on our time and different preferences for sharing and separateness. So the 'relationship dance' becomes a vital way of navigating space and negotiating compromises, even when it isn't spoken out loud between us. It's also an important way in which we demonstrate how well we know and understand each other. We'll come back to this idea that communication is often unspoken in the next chapter.

SUMMARY SUGGESTIONS: ON THE HOME FRONT

Here are a few more things to try yourself, based on this chapter.

- Imagine your ideal home. What would it look like? Would you live in it alone, or with others? Try to let your imagination go wherever it wants rather than feeling like there's a way of living you *should* choose. How close is your current situation to this? Are there ways that you could get closer to this ideal even within the limits that you have? Perhaps the examples you've read about in this chapter give you some ideas you'd like to try out.
- What does home mean to you? How important is it? What do you want from home? What have your good and bad experiences of home been in the past? Try talking about this with a partner or friend. They may well have very different understandings of home.
- Create an emotion map. Consider the parts of your home that are comfort zones and hot spots for you.
- Ask your partner or friend to join you in a shared TV session or a home dance. This might be something spontaneous, or you can deliberately think about what you'd each like from the situation and how you might negotiate something that meets both your preferences.

CHAPTER 3
IT'S NOT WHAT YOU SAY...

*Whatever words we utter should be chosen with care
for people will hear them and be influenced by them for
good or ill – Buddha*

We're dedicating this whole chapter to communication because we found that it was a major linchpin in enduring love. However what we learnt about the role of communication in relationships wasn't necessarily what you'd expect, as you'll see.

Before we start have a go at this quiz to help you pin down the positive and negative aspects of your own relationship.

QUIZ TIME: WHAT YOU LIKE BEST AND LEAST IN YOUR RELATIONSHIP

Answer the following questions about your current relationship. If you're not in a relationship, think back to a previous relationship or one that you imagine being in in the future.

1. Say two things that you like *best* about your relationship.

_____

_____

2. Say two things that you like *least* about your relationship.

_____

_____

The reason we've included these questions here is that, in our study, the most common answers that people gave were about communication. Many people said the things they liked *best* about their relationship were positive forms of communication, and that arguments and problems with communication were the things they liked *least* of all. Did communication feature in your answers to these questions?

VITAL STATISTICS:

What do you like best and least about your relationship?

These are the top ten answers given by people in our research:

What I like best:
1. Laughing together
2. Sharing values and interests
3. Being best friends
4. Being cared for, and feeling supported
5. Feeling safe and secure
6. Being happy
7. Trust
8. Sharing a close relationship
9. Talking and listening
10. Being in love and/or being loved

What I like least
1. Poor communication
2. Arguments and/or conflicts
3. Housework and/or childcare not shared fairly
4. Issues with balancing work and home life
5. Few shared values and/or interests
6. Not enough couple time
7. Money issues
8. Living apart and/or housing issues
9. Different needs or expectations around sexual intimacy
10. Lack of closeness

So you can see that communication came right at the top of both lists. In combination, poor communication and arguments are by far the top things that people like least about their relationships. And the thing that they like best is laughing together, which is certainly a form of communication. Talking and listening are also on the list of things people like best, and you might also remember, from Chapter 1, that these were one of the five main ways in which people feel appreciated by a partner.

Many of the other things that people like best and least about their relationships involve communication indirectly. For example, sharing values, being best friends, feeling supported, and trusting each other are all things that people experience and express through conversations where they listen to each other and show their understanding. Also, many of the things that people like least are causes of arguments, such as money problems, work–home balance, and housework. We'll be covering all of these things in the rest of this chapter.

Talking and listening

While we were writing this book a piece of relationship research hit the headlines. A *New York Times* article came out which made the grand claim that readers could 'fall in love with anyone' if they followed their advice.

The article was based on a study that psychologist Arthur Aron and his colleagues carried out 20 years ago. They wanted to find out whether disclosing personal details made people feel closer to each other. So they got pairs of strangers in a laboratory to ask each other 36 increasingly intimate questions. Apparently two of the participants fell in love with each other because of taking part in the experiment!

New York Times journalist Mandy Len Catron decided to repeat the study with a friend of hers. She describes how they had a long conversation, based around the questions from the experiment, and this resulted in them falling in love too.

Before long people were talking about the article all over social media, sharing the 36 questions, and writing parody versions of them.

TRY IT YOURSELF: 36 QUESTIONS

You can try this out for yourself with a partner or friend. It's certainly an interesting way of finding out what you already know about somebody, and what you don't. It might also be helpful for building empathy and seeing them as a whole person, something we'll come back to later in the chapter.

The idea is to have three blocks of twelve questions which get increasingly personal. So the first block begins to establish what makes you tick: the kind of things you like doing, what you'd do on your perfect day, and a four-minute summary of your life. The second block probes a bit deeper and includes questions about how you feel towards your family and friends, and your most treasured and terrible memories. The third block aims to get up close and personal by asking questions like when you last cried, and what secrets you have. There are also some questions about what you think you have in common, and what you like best about each other, having had this conversation.

If you want to test the experiment yourself we've included the original 36 questions at the end of the book. Alternatively, you could come up with your own sets of questions, based on what you'd find most interesting to ask and answer.

From the 36 questions experiment it certainly seems that communication can be extremely powerful in relationships. Talking intimately with each other can increase our feelings of closeness and – if we believe the hype – it might even be able to make us fall in love. Relationship advice also often focuses on getting partners to communicate more: talking about their relationships with each other and – if that doesn't work – talking together with a specialist like a relationship therapist.

Both the 36 questions, and talking with a therapist, involve speaking about things that we don't often say, or that we've stopped talking about over time. So what we communicate about is at least as important as the fact that we communicate. It's often about discussing things that give us a greater *understanding* of each other.

Given the importance placed on communication in relationships we weren't all that surprised about the fact that people in our study prioritised it. However, we were surprised by what a lot of them *meant* by communication. Often they didn't mean the kind of 'big talk' involved in the 36 questions research, or the kind of conversations suggested by relationship advisors and therapists. Instead, they were talking about much more everyday conversations, and the kinds of communication that don't require the spoken word.

Talking about the relationship

We'll start here with people who said that it *was* important for them to talk about their relationship with their partner, and to discuss how they felt about it. However, keep in mind that these people were actually in the minority when it came to the kind of communication that people valued most.

> 'She communicates really well with me so I'm always aware of how she is feeling.'

> 'He makes me feel like I can tell him anything really. He's so open about his feelings, he never hides anything from me and when he tries to he ends up telling me about it in this very cute way of his.'

Rob felt that having open conversations in his relationship with Ed was vital, however uncomfortable it felt, because it built trust between the two of them.

> 'Even if I felt uncomfortable about talking about it I would talk about it because I said to Ed, "no matter how uncomfortable you feel, or how embarrassing something might be, or how bad you feel, we should always talk about things"'.

For Rob and Ed it's important to know how the other person's feeling even if it's difficult or stressful for them to express it. Their ongoing relationship conversation reassures them that they can tackle problems head on, as and when they crop up, rather than storing them up for the future.

Other people emphasised self-disclosure because they feel that 'deep knowing' is a key part of a loving relationship. For these people, partnership is a special kind of relationship, because you share intimate knowledge about each other that you might hold back with a friend or family member, for example. Of course, not everybody makes these distinctions, and others share more with friends and family than they do with partners.

For some people learning more about themselves is one reason why they even *have* partner relationships. They appreciate deep conversations as a kind of *personal growth*: 'She's taught me things about myself and I recognise a lot more of what I'm like.'

Think about where you stand on this. Is big talk important in your relationships or would you prefer a relationship without too much self-examination? Would you be more likely to share intimate details with a partner or with other people in your life?

While full disclosure was important for some people, as we previously mentioned most people value everyday conversations more than big relationship discussions.

Everyday talk and listening

The type of talk that seems to be most important to people is the kind where they tell each other about their days, chatting about inconsequential things and mulling over the minutiae of their lives. In these kinds of conversations reciprocation is definitely vital. That means it's important to be able to talk and *be listened to*, and vice versa.

> 'My partner always talks to me and listens when I feel the need to talk and to be heard.'

> 'Listens to me and makes me feel understood and cared about.'

People generally like to feel involved in their partners' lives, and to feel that partners are interested in theirs. Again, some people felt that their relationship was special because their partner was the *only* person who they told these everyday details to. In her diary Zoe wrote about how she and her partner talk to each other about their everyday problems and how to tackle them.

> 'Charlotte arrived home soon after six and "debriefed" about some difficult conversations she'd had in the afternoon with project funders. She often does that, and I hope it was helpful. I don't know a lot about the details but I try and be a sounding board when she needs to talk something through.'

This kind of debrief allows partners to share parts of their life, such as work, which might otherwise be unfamiliar or kept outside their relationship. We often spend a great deal of our lives at work, so sharing this side of ourselves with a partner can help break down the divide between our work lives and home lives.

For people like Zoe and Charlotte, the relationship can be a safe 'sounding board', a space where they test out their ideas and thoughts before going public. A short 'debrief' about work at the start of the evening can be a way of putting away the stresses of the day before settling into their down-time together.

People differ over what they're looking for from these kinds of conversations. For example, some people just want to be listened to, while others want practical help from a partner. We'll come back to some of these differences towards the end of the chapter, but for now think about what you're hoping for when you talk about your day with somebody close. Consider whether you do any kind of debrief between work time and home time. If so, what's its purpose, for you and for the other person?

Whatever their reasons for debriefing like this, people put a lot of emphasis on *sharing* their lives:

'Sharing all our problems with one another.'

'Talking to each other, hearing each other's news, sharing worries.'

'We talk every day, and share all of our problems with one another.'

For many people, it isn't so much *what* they talk about that's important; it's more the familiarity and closeness of *sharing a conversation* that matters. Moira linked everyday conversation to the sorts of shared activities that we covered in Chapter 1:

'We like to go out with each other and just get involved in other things and then come back and talk. We talk a lot to each other about all sorts of things. We watch telly occasionally and just talk about it. We're interested in what the other might have to say about things. I think that's really been a cement and a joy in our relationship.'

This kind of conversation is an important way for many people of keeping their relationships alive and vibrant, as well as bonding them together. Now we'll explore another kind of everyday communication which does a similar thing.

Laughter and banter

As you saw in the vital statistics earlier, laughing together was the thing that people generally liked the very best about their relationships. Like dancing together, which we covered in the last chapter, laughing together is something that people often remember with great pleasure when they talk about their relationships.

'We laugh a lot and bring out the best in each other.'

'We laugh at ourselves and each other.'

What people love about these moments is the way that they *spontaneously erupt* in their everyday lives, jolting them out of the ordinary for a little while and enabling them to live in the moment. We know from research on mindfulness that 'being present' or 'in the moment' is great for our happiness and well-being. Laughter can be a short-cut to a mindful moment when most of us spend so much of our lives mulling over the past or planning the future.

Laughing together also has lots of different meanings for people. Like the debrief chat at the end of the day, laughter can be an escape from the everyday strains of life. Having a good laugh together is a great form of stress-relief. Laughing can also be a sign of closeness in a relationship: the fact that we laugh at similar things or know exactly what to say in order to tickle our partner's funny bone.

Related to laughter, banter can be a useful way of avoiding, or managing, conflict for some people. You can tease each other out of an argument: saying something that you know will raise a smile to diffuse a difficult moment. Sensing how far

TOP TIP

Have a go at creating space for a laughing moment with a partner or somebody else in your life. Start by thinking about the role of laughter in your relationship. Is it something that features? If so, when does it tend to happen?

If the answers to this are easy you might well find it simple to create such a moment: it'll only take putting on that YouTube clip that tickles you both, reminding the other person of a funny memory, or saying the word that always makes you crack up.

If laughing isn't so familiar to you, you might go for watching a movie or comedian who makes you both chuckle. Or you could try the trick of just starting to laugh. People who teach 'laughing yoga' have found that actually making yourselves laugh often becomes so ridiculous that you end up laughing for real. Sometimes people lie on the floor to do it, or even rest their heads on each other's bellies!

Afterwards reflect on what laughing means to you and whether it's something you'd like to build more space for in your relationship.

you can push a joke with a partner can be another clear sign of 'deep knowing' because, of course, what is fond teasing in one relationship might feel barbed and bullying in another, or even at different times in the same relationship.

We often found that laughter happened when partners reminisced together over incidents in their lives. For example, Tony and Sophie shared the story of when they got engaged, laughing most of the way through it.

Tony: I always feel for people who get engaged on a beach in the Caribbean because how often are you going to be able to go back there and reminisce about it?

Sophie: Yes! But we can always go back to windy Wales. How many times have you been on Facebook and someone's getting engaged in New York or Paris? I'm glad you didn't do anything like that because I'd just find that really cheesy!

Tony: I bet you're so glad I didn't take you to New York! I can't think of anything worse!

Sophie: But as a story, it's a good one in comparison to some of my friends, or just going to a restaurant.

Tony: Yes. I'm glad it's something I'll never have to do again!

Sophie: Why? Did you think I'd say, 'no' and push you over the aqueduct?

Tony: Oh no, I knew you'd be a 'yes'.

Sophie: Oh really?!

In Chapter 6 we'll say more at how partners often tell these kinds of relationship stories together as a way of reinforcing the bonds between them, often with lots of jokes and laughter thrown in. Are there any memories that you return to like this in your relationships?

Communicating without talking

Of course, laughing together doesn't always involve words. It's often more about catching each other's eye when something reminds you of a private joke, or collapsing into giggles over something that one of your kids or pets does.

Like this, many of the most highly valued forms of communication don't involve talking at all. Non-verbal communication and silences are often equally precious. They can speak volumes, saying more than spoken words could ever hope to articulate.

More than words

Like laughter, silence has many different meanings for people, depending on what being quiet meant in their families growing up, for example; or the role that it plays in their relationship now.

For some of us, silence feels like a punishment or a sign that someone is disapproving of us, judging us, or deliberately 'shutting us out'. If there's an 'awkward pause' in conversation some of us find it unsettling and rush to fill it with chatter. For others, going quiet is a sign that we're taking somebody seriously and trying to really hear what they're saying. It may be that we're a slow and reflective type of person who needs regular pauses in order to digest information. Some of us find that still moments are when we feel closest to our partner, or that our partner is the only person in our lives that we do feel able to have comfortable silences with. Looking into each other's eyes or holding each other can sometimes do away with the need for words. Talking at all at such times might spoil the moment.

For some people taking time out to just be together quietly is very precious. It doesn't need to be a special occasion. In her diary, Ann nicely sums up how important it is for her and Tom to get some quiet time away from their two-year-old son. Silence can indeed be golden for parents!

> *'We walked into the cafe and I asked Tom to get some papers to read. Tom said, "I thought we've come to talk to each other." I said. "No, read the papers." We both laughed! I had a coffee and Tom had a beer. We sat reading magazines enjoying some time to relax together without Ollie.'*

Some partners learn the different meanings that they have around silence very well, and others remain confused about them. Think about how you feel about silence, and what you tend to assume if a partner goes quiet. In her interview, Ella spoke about how she'd learnt to understand her partner Russell's moments of silent withdrawal and to navigate them differently at different times. She said to Russell:

> *'You don't realise you're doing it, but you're naturally very introvert.*

'Sometimes I leave him and let him have space and then there's other times where it's like, I have to draw him back out again: "come back, come back!" And actually when he's like that, he doesn't talk, there's no cuddles. He does literally just go into himself.
'But then that's you isn't it?'

Ella went on to say that, for her, this deep knowledge of how Russell works is a fundamental part of being in a long-term relationship with him. Ella and Russell met through online dating in their mid-fifties after the break-up of both of their previous marriages. Their mutual acceptance and understanding distinguished their current partnership from their previous – painful – relationships.

Similarly, Margaret and Martin had learnt that time away from communication with each other could be just as important as time spent chatting together. At such times they could make independent decisions which the other person might come to appreciate.

Margaret: Oh it's so funny because I remember, Martin, you were quite keen on getting gadgets, like a dishwasher and a microwave in the kitchen. And I said 'no, no, don't need it.' But then I went away to Holland and when I got back all of a sudden there's a dishwasher installed. And I said 'oh this is quite good!' So the microwave was installed at once!

Martin (mimicking Margaret): 'We don't need that. Oh yes it's quite good actually!'

Of course, remembering back to Chapter 2, the spaces that people live in, and who they share them with, can have a big impact on what kinds of communication are possible. Silence can become a valuable commodity for partners who live with a large family, or a painful pressure between partners who've lived together for years and can no longer find much to say to each other. Shahnaaz and Michael, for example, spoke about how they had to communicate quietly when they lived with Shanaaz's parents. It was a big relief to move into their own space where they could find the kinds of communication which fitted them, rather than basing it around somebody else's preferences.

QUIZ TIME: ARE YOU OKAY WITH SILENCE?

Answer the following questions:

1. Do you like to always have a TV or radio on, or music playing in the background? Yes/No
2. If you're with another person, does being quiet make you uncomfortable? Yes/No
3. Would you say that you need at least 30 minutes of quiet alone-time each day? Yes/No
4. Do you find silence relaxing? Yes/No
5. Are there several people in your life who you can happily sit with quietly? Yes/No
6. If you went out for a meal and nobody was talking much would you find it stressful? Yes/No
7. Does the idea of going on a silent retreat fill you with horror? Yes/No
8. Try sitting in silence for a minute with your eyes shut now. Did you find it peaceful? Yes/No

How Did You Score?

For questions 1, 2, 6 and 7, give yourself a point if you said 'Yes'. For questions 3, 4, 5 and 8 give yourself a point if you said 'No'. Tot up your total score

6 or more: You really hate silence! You'd much rather that there was a babble of sound going on around you and that people were talking.

---

2 or less: You love the quiet! Generally speaking you prefer still environments and companionable silences to lots of noise and chatter.

3-5: You're somewhere in the middle. You like being quiet in some situations but not all the time. Maybe you're happier with silence if somebody else is around, or if you're on your own.

If you're happy where you are, no problem. You might want to let people in your life know though so that they understand what'd going on when you seem uncomfortable during a lull in conversation, or when you say you're craving some peace.

If you'd like to become more relaxed with silence then it's worth thinking about what it means to you, and reminding yourself that it can have other meanings. Also you can practise spending a little time a day – alone and/or with a partner – deliberately being quiet, to get more familiar with it.

Virtual communication

As we saw in the last chapter, by no means all partners live together, and many don't have a lot of everyday time together for communicating. In these kinds of relationships, texts, online messages and phone-calls often became relationship lifelines.

Long-distance partnerships particularly need to develop different ways of having conversations, banter, and communication without words, because these things can't always happen in person. For example, many people in long distance-relationships pepper the day with brief message exchanges, or pictures of where they are, in order to bridge the geographical gap. Pillow talk can involve falling asleep with the other person virtually next to you on Skype or FaceTime.

Where do you stand on everyday virtual communication in a relationship? Is it something you like, or do you prefer only face-to-face contact?

As with offline communication, the emphasis in online contact is often on touching base with each other and having everyday chatter rather than lengthy conversations or big talk. Like the love notes that we mentioned in Chapter 1, people find that short phone calls or computer messages are valuable ways of demonstrating their love and appreciation. For example, they say things like:

> *'She sends texts for no reason other than to say she is thinking of me.'*

> *'I appreciate them calling or texting to share something with me.'*

In her research diary, Abigail included the following image:

She said:

'I receive a daily cartoon by email. I forwarded yesterday's cartoon via email to my partner adding an emoticon heart. He replied this morning with an emoticon kiss and hug!'

Think about whether you have a preference for the kinds of virtual contact that you prefer. For example, would you rather be able to see the other person, hear them, or do you prefer writing? Do you like to be communicating at the same time – like online chat or phone calls – or do you prefer to receive a message and have time to respond at a different point?

For some people, emails and messages can also be a safer way to have heart-to-heart conversations about things that are difficult to communicate about in person. However, not many people prefer this. There's a general sense that it can be too easy to misunderstand each other in online conversations because you can't see the other person's face or body language. Of course, people have different preferences depending on how familiar they are with online communication, for example, or whether they express themselves better in writing or face-to-face. What's this like for you? Is virtual contact something you find useful for big conversations or only for small talk?

Virtual communication feels different at different points in a relationship as well. A surprise text message can send your heart fluttering in the early stages of a relationship. In a long-term relationship it can give you a warm glow that your partner still thinks about you when you're apart. Or it can feel like an uncomfortable interruption if it reminds you about an ongoing argument you're having with a partner in the middle of your workday. It can even become an unbearable pressure if you have a partner who wants a lot more contact than you do.

Like other forms of communication, online communication has the potential both to endanger people's relationships and to enrich them. In fact, perhaps this is particularly the case with online communication because most of us are still getting used to a world with smartphones and easy Internet access.

We found that dating websites and social networking had a positive role for many people in getting together with their partner. Lots of people also said that everyday online contact helped them to feel 'held in mind' in their relationship. However, equal numbers of people spoke of how constant use of smartphones and laptops became a barrier between themselves and their partner. Others said that the potential for having sex and relationships online felt like a constant threat to their partnership. Here we'll just give a couple of longer examples of what the Internet opened up, and what it closed down, for people's relationships.

In their interview, Anne and Henry revealed that social media was what got them together in the first place.

> **Anne:** It started when I got to chat a bit with you on Facebook.
>
> **Henry:** I'm of the modern English school of courtship where you go out and get very, very drunk and stumble into someone in a nightclub. It might be a one-night stand that turns into something more significant. I think when I met you I was still in that kind of frame of mind. I don't want to over-attribute things to Facebook. It sounds trivial, but I think that it allowed our relationship, because we chatted online and it was a bit more civilised.

Seeing each other's everyday lives on social networking sites and getting to know each other over instant messaging can be the equivalent to the 36 questions experiment for some people. Social networking gives us one way of gradually self-disclosing and becoming closer before getting together in person.

However, Peter spoke about how his Internet activity had become a very difficult issue in his relationship, particularly in relation to his enjoyment of online pornography. This wasn't so much because of the pornography itself, but because it was so difficult to talk about openly and honestly with his partner, eroding the trust between them.

'I don't want to upset her any more. I do love her so much. I really, really care and I hate myself for being the way I am. She says it's more than the actual watching or downloading. It's more about the lies. But I would lie because I felt ashamed of who I am and what I do. I didn't want her to know about it because I didn't want to jeopardise our love life and our sex life as well. It hurt a lot because I knew I was lying to her. But I was lying to protect her feelings and also so she didn't judge me.'

Think, yourself, about these two examples. How do you feel about the prospect of starting a relationship online, or about having some of your sex life online? Both of these scenarios involve negotiation and trust, albeit in different ways perhaps.

It's important to remember that these two examples of good and bad online experiences could equally work the other way around. For some people, the experience of being on social media could be a negative one. You might constantly compare yourself with the seemingly perfect lives of others, feeling increasingly anxious and therefore less able to enjoy getting to know people in the relaxed way that Henry and Anne describe. For other people, engaging with online erotica is a positive experience. It might be something which a person enjoys sharing with a partner as part of their sex life, or a way of meeting sexual desires that they have which don't interest their partner. We'll return to some of these ideas in the next chapter.

As Peter's experience suggests, the key issue may be more about *how* people engage with online communication rather than *what* they actually do online. If the Internet disrupts everyday communication, takes away valuable aspects of a relationship or brings up points of serious disagreement, then it's likely to feel negative and hard to communicate openly about. However, if it offers the potential to enrich and expand the existing relationship then it can feel like a positive thing that people want to explore further.

Arguments and bickering

As we saw earlier, conflicts and breakdowns in communication, like the one between Peter and his partner, are top of the list of things that people like least about their relationships. Also, many of the other items on that list are common causes of arguments and disagreements, including housework and childcare, the home–work balance, getting time together, money issues, housing difficulties, and having different sexual desires.

Perhaps the most vital thing to remember about conflict is that it's absolutely inevitable in close relationships. We often get the impression from the media that 'perfect' relationships exist which are argument-free. Actually, as psychologists Carol Tavris and Elliot Aronson point out in their book on conflict, it's impossible to be close to somebody without falling out at times. There's no way you'll agree on everything and sometimes you're bound to come up against problems that are difficult to resolve. Some of these will probably cause ongoing conflicts that crop up from time to time in your relationship. You'll also see each other at your most vulnerable and that can be a very tough thing to deal with when it happens.

What do partners come in conflict about?

People fall out over all kinds of different things but some types of argument become more sticky and hard to handle than others. We found that people don't generally mind too much when they disagree over their views or opinions, those are often the topics of a kind of 'positive conflict' that we'll come to later. 'Negative conflicts' are more often about major inequalities between partners, and these are also often much harder to resolve.

The main two points of conflict which came up again and again in our research were about inequalities in domestic chores or childcare, and money. These conflicts mostly happened between partners who were in male–female relationships where there was some expectation that they would conform to 'traditional' gender roles. This typically boiled down to the woman being expected to do most of the housework and childcare, and the man earning and/or controlling the money.

People struggled particularly if one partner expected a more equal division of labour and the other didn't. For example, it became difficult if both partners worked but the woman was expected to shoulder the double burden of employment and childcare, or if domestic work was not seen as work and appreciated in the same way as paid employment. These were the kinds of things that women said they liked least about their relationships.

> *'Unequal share of housework and children stuff – no matter how many hints I drop.'*

> *'The relationship is really one-sided. I work, look after the kids and do all the housework, etc.'*

Thinking back to Chapter 1 you can see that this is the flipside of the kinds of things that other people appreciated about their relationships. People spoke very positively about partners who 'did more than their fair share', looking after children even though they worked full-time, or doing chores that they knew their partner hated.

Similarly, although around three-quarters of people felt that their financial resources were fairly distributed and didn't argue about money, there were some serious tensions in households where one person – usually a male partner – had greater control over the finances. People in this situation listed the following as the things they liked least about their relationships:

> *'His reluctance to talk about money.'*

> *'Communication about finances – husband is secretive about money and I find it frustrating.'*

'Having to ask before making a big purchase.'

'He is tight with money!'

Like housework and childcare, these things can be a painful reminder to women of the gender inequalities which still exist on a wider scale in society. The pay gap between men and women remains at just under 10 per cent. Women are more likely to be in part-time work, and are expected to take responsibility for organising the bulk of child-rearing. Women in such situations can feel an overwhelming sense of anger and unfairness, but also a sense of powerlessness because wider society seems to support these inequalities. Unfortunately we don't have the space to go into this in a lot of detail here, but if you do feel this tension we've included a couple of books by Laurie Penny and Harriet Lerner that you might find helpful in the reading list at the end of this book.

We also heard about how some men really struggled when the 'traditional' role of breadwinner wasn't available to them due to difficulties finding employment or ill-health, for example. Patrick said that he felt weak and useless when he couldn't contribute financially in his relationship. While his situation has now changed for the better, at the time the financial circumstances – and how they made him *feel* – were a major source of friction between him and his partner.

However, other men found that they were able to navigate shifting gender roles more easily. Nick, for example, ensured that all of the jobseeker allowance went to his partner to pay for the house and kids, and he was proud of the fact that they didn't argue about money.

Financial constraints are often linked to housing issues. In such circumstances the physical situation that partners find themselves in can really impact on the kind of conflicts they have. Greg, for example, commented that unemployment had caused tensions between him and his partner because they didn't get any time apart in their cramped flat, with no jobs to go to:

'We've got nothing to talk about because we've been with each other all day. And, of course, because you've been together all day you can wind each other up.'

While it's definitely true that women in our study did more than their fair share of housework, men often did help out and – if you recall Theo in Chapter 1 – some of them took on the main domestic role in the partnership. This didn't mean that arguments about housework simply disappeared, but it did influence how they played out. Robert, for example, previously ran a business from home and did most of his chores during the daytime in his breaks from work. Now circumstances have changed and Robert goes into an office, so the only times available for him to do chores are evenings and weekends. This has caused conflict between him and his partner because they can't agree on how to do the housework. She likes them to do chores together whereas he'd rather divide up the tasks between them.

It also doesn't seem to matter how big your shared space is, whether you feel constantly on top of each other or are used to a larger area. Even though partners with disposable income could afford to resolve domestic conflicts by having separate rooms, or by employing a cleaner, housework and childcare responsibilities often remained a source of tension between them.

So you can see that relationships don't happen in a vacuum: wider social ideas and inequalities often play out between partners, and external situations can make it likely that conflict will occur. It may be helpful to think about your own expectations around these areas. Do you tend to assume that people will have certain roles in your relationship? Is this related to gender roles in the wider society at all, or are you bucking the trend?

Problems often arise when people assume that their partners will see things the same way that they do, and then find out that they actually don't. Think about where you stand on sharing domestic chores, for example, and on finance. We touched on these issues in the quiz at the start of Chapter 2 so you could think back to your answers there, and how important it is – for you – that a partner shares those views. We'll come to how to communicate about these kinds of things shortly.

Stuck patterns and escalation

Like other people who've researched relationship conflict, we found that certain patterns became stuck in relationships, leading to pain on all sides when they played out more and more often. For example, people said things like:

'We argue too easily and it always gets blown up out of all proportion as a result of not listening to each other.'

'We often have problems resolving conflicts/ending fights.'

Psychologists Carol Tavris and Elliot Aronson, who we mentioned earlier, found that a root cause of a good deal of relationship conflict is the strong belief that we're right and the other person is wrong. This comes across quite clearly in the following answer to our 'what do you like least in your relationship?' question!

'Her utter inability to stack the dishwasher.'

From seemingly inconsequential niggles like stacking the dishwasher, to bigger issues about how to manage money, where to live, or how to have sex, if each partner is convinced that they're right and the other person is wrong, the conflict is likely to escalate. Both people defend and justify themselves, and dismiss and reject their partner, and that results in the kind of vicious cycle which most of us fall into from time to time.

With disagreements it's useful to shift from the common idea that there are right and wrong answers, to recognising that there are multiple valid perspectives. This isn't easy, but it opens up far more possible avenues to explore:

- It might be that one of you moves closer to the other's position.
- You may reach a compromise.
- You might agree to differ, respecting that you have different points of view. This involves recognising that all relationships have some areas of disagreement and this is just one of yours that will inevitably bubble up from time to time.
- It might be that this is a difference which is too hard to live with and requires some bigger kind of change in the relationship; but it's still no one person's 'fault'.

Empathy is key here. If you think back to some of the earlier examples we gave, Ella was okay with Russell's tendency to withdraw from her because she'd learnt to appreciate that that was just how he was. Margaret welcomed Martin's independent decision to buy a dishwasher even though it wasn't what she'd wanted, because she could understand why he'd done it. Both of these issues *could* become causes of serious conflict in a relationship – and do in other relationships – but they didn't here because Ella and Margaret were able to empathise with Russell and Martin: to see things from their perspectives.

Most relationship therapy is all about helping partners to put themselves in each other's shoes. Sometimes it can get to the point where you need an outside person to help you to do this because you're so caught up in the situation yourself that you can't see it clearly. However, there are things you can try for yourself.

As we saw with the 36 questions, this kind of activity is a good way of reminding yourself that a partner sees the world in a different way to you, and that's okay. Anything where you try to see each other with fresh eyes is helpful, such as making the kind of us-time we spoke about in Chapter 1.

TOP TIP

To build empathy about a particular conflict try explaining an argument from your partner's point of view to a friend, or in writing.

Or make time with a partner to discuss a disagreement (nothing too major!) when you give each other ten minutes to really listen to the other's point of view, then feedback what you heard from their perspective. The aim of the conversation is just to understand each other's position as fully as possible, not to come to any conclusion.

Reflect afterwards on what it's like to shift the goal of this kind of communication from winning or resolving the conflict to reaching a better understanding of where the other person is coming from.

Psychologists agree that it's worth taking time out alone before embarking on this kind of conversation because it's much harder to see the other person's perspective when you're angry. If anger does bubble up it's best – although not always easy – to step away and to come back when you're calmer.

Positive conflict and bickering

This point about empathy leads us to the idea that conflicts are not necessarily a bad thing, especially if they lead to greater understanding between people. Partners who accept that there will inevitably be some conflict in their relationship actually often see it as a positive feature. For example:

'Because we grapple with our disagreements, we make sense of the world and we both make compromises – at times struggle is part of a good relationship.'

Conflict can result in more or less intimacy between people, depending on how it plays out. For example, it can feel unbearable to be seen at your worst by a partner during a row and to feel rejected by them. But it can equally be amazing to reach that breaking point and to know that your partner still loves and accepts you afterwards. People who can bear the conflict in their relationships often feel that they're stronger for it, and that it improves their capacity to communicate.

Emmie and Theo are a good example of a couple who feel that they learnt from their conflicts:

> **Emmie:** We're self-aware enough that even if we reach a point where we scream at each other, half an hour later we realise that that's actually nothing to do with each other, or if it is we'd sit down and we talk it through. So we always try and resolve things within about two or three hours.
>
> **Theo:** I don't think we've ever been mad at each other for more than a couple of hours.

Another kind of conflict that can be positive is bickering. While some people see this as a 'bad sign' in a relationship or find it irritating, others enjoy back-and-forth banter and even feel that they get closer to each other through letting off steam like this. As we said earlier, teasing and bickering can be a good way of demonstrating how well you know each other.

Louise described how her friends and family have a very different view on bickering than she does. For her and Luke mutual 'snipping' is a good thing. Their playful banter even cropped up in their interview!

> **Louise:** We really annoy everybody. My sister gets so annoyed by it: Luke popped home yesterday, and we were having a little snip at each other and my sister's like 'I'm going home. If you argue about one more thing, I'm leaving.'
>
> **Luke:** I wasn't arguing!

Clearly people have very different ideas about what counts as arguing, bickering, or conflict. You might remember from Chapter 1 that the psychologist John Gottman found that strong relationships could be high in conflict or low in conflict, or anything in between. The thing that's important – whether the relationship is fiery or calm – is that there are far more appreciative interactions than there are critical ones.

It comes back, again, to the fact that different people have different meanings around all kinds of communication. As with laughter and silence, we receive different messages about conflict when we're growing up, and from the culture around us. So, for some of us, a raised voice is terrifying, while for others it's just part of the cut-and-thrust of everyday banter. Some of us prefer a lot of emotional expression, whereas others prefer things to stay on a pretty even keel. One person might have the rule 'never go to sleep on an argument', while their partner might need a couple of days to process things before returning to a disagreement.

Have a think for yourself where you stand on these matters. Do you like a relationship that's hot and fiery, cool and calm, or somewhere in between? What are your preferences for dealing with disagreements? These will be useful points to hold onto for the final section. Partners who have very different expectations and preferences about communication struggle most, so we'll turn to this to bring the chapter to a close.

Meta-communication

Meta-communication means communicating about communicating. Basically it's all about recognising that we have our own personal ideas about how we like to communicate, and that some communication styles come more easily to us than others. As we saw with the examples of laughter, silence and raised voices, all forms of communication have different meanings for different people.

Instead of trying to impose our way of communicating onto another person – 'I'm right and you're wrong' – meta-communication is about figuring out between you how you're going to communicate. This involves being up for understanding where the other person is coming from, and being aware that the messages they've learnt about communication growing up may be different from your own. As one person in our study put it: *'We have different communication styles, but we both work hard at it.'*

Differences in communication styles mean that it's often useful to talk about how we communicate before even getting into a conversation! Counsellors and therapists refer to this as a focus on *process* rather than *content*. When we're dealing with the *process* of communication we're talking about *how* we communicate. That means we can then go into the *content* of communication with an awareness of this. If the discussion of content becomes difficult it can often be useful to return to talking about the process (How are we communicating here? Is it working for us?), before getting back into the content.

This is important because different ways of communicating are more or less comfortable or familiar to different people. It depends on all kinds of aspects, such as a person's cultural or class background, age, the generation they grew up in, and so on.

A couple of good examples are talking over the top of each other and eye contact. Some families show that they're interested in what each other have to say by interrupting all the time, whereas others show the same thing by quietly and patiently waiting their turn. In some cultures direct eye contact is a sign that you're listening to somebody or taking them seriously, in others it's a sign of disrespect or hostility.

In her diary, Debs gave a great example of how their family have developed a communication style which works for them, but which would be baffling to anybody observing them:

'The kids invented the concept of "interminding" for when you interrupt someone but they don't mind because you read their mind. Thinking about it now, Joss and I do this a lot to each other – we have conversations that must be completely incomprehensible because sentences and thoughts are not completed and we talk over each other but are still listening.'

How we prefer to communicate

A great starting point for 'communicating about communicating' is to consider how aspects like our culture, class, gender, age, generation, disability, sexuality, religion, etc. impact on how we communicate. Consider questions like:

- How did the people around you communicate when you were growing up? Who was included or excluded from interactions? What styles of verbal and non-verbal communication did people use? Which ones were more or less approved of or successful? What did you like or dislike about this? Have any of these family patterns impacted on your communication styles today?
- Are there any aspects of how your particular body and/or mind works which mean that certain ways of communicating are easier or more difficult for you?
- What expectations do you think there are on how people of your gender, race, class, age, body type, religion, cultural background, or sexuality communicate? Do any of these fit your preferred way of communicating? Do any of them feel uncomfortable or awkward?

Try remembering an interaction which you really didn't like and one you really did like in recent weeks. What do the differences between these tell you about your preferred way of communicating? Do you have any hard limits, such as ways of communicating that absolutely do *not* feel okay? Do you have any strong preferences for how you *like* to communicate? Are there aspects you're willing to compromise on?

It can also be useful to think about the specifics of our communication preferences, given how many different forms of communication are available to us. For example, think about whether you prefer to communicate about something:

- Straight away, or after having some time to think
- Verbally or in a written form (such as email, text and online chat)

- Face-to-face or at a distance, via Internet or telephone
- At particular times of day (for example 'not before I've had my morning coffee', or 'not last thing at night when you're tired')
- At home or someplace neutral
- In private or with other people around

Also consider whether some spaces are simply too intimate and intense to have a conversation, such as when you're in the bath. Or maybe those feel like particularly relaxed places where conversations flow most freely.

What are we aiming at?

There are lots of different things that we might want to happen when we communicate with a partner. Given how many conflicts occur simply because people are looking for different things out of an interaction, it can be very useful to discuss what we're hoping to achieve before getting into the conversation itself. Thinking back to an earlier example from this chapter, Zoe seemed to realise that her partner Charlotte just wanted a sounding board and didn't need her to help with the situation. Anne and Henry gave a similar example:

Anne: I think a lot of the time you know what you're doing. You probably just like to let me know what's going on, so you tell me.

Henry: I do quite a lot of thinking out loud.

Anne: It's not like you need my opinion, I'm just listening.

Other people, however, clearly want more input. They hope that conversations with a partner will move forward their own thinking, or give them an alternative viewpoint that might be useful to hear, for example: '*I love talking to my wife and getting her insight.*'

Anne and Henry, and Zoe and Charlotte, have reached an understanding and know the purpose of conversations between them. But there are often times of miscommunication when we want different things. For example, we just want someone to sympathise with us, but our partner assumes that we want advice. Or we're just enjoying making a connection, but our partner assumes there should be some definite outcome to the conversation. Or we really want some practical support, but our partner thinks it'd be best to just keep listening. It depends on the topic of conversation, of course. We might want our partner to listen to us and have some input if we're talking about getting married, whereas we'd probably be happier for them to be a sounding board if we just want to ramble about work for a bit.

Importantly, it's not about prioritising certain kinds of communication over others, but rather about a collaborative process of finding the best communication style for you and your partner, and for the aims that you have in any given conversation.

The list below gives some typical aims of communication. You can also add your own examples to this list. Think about which ones you're looking for in general, and from a specific conversation.

Possible aims of communication include:

- To make a connection
- To impart information
- To find out information
- To get support
- To problem solve
- To make a decision
- To persuade
- To discuss
- To get a response
- To think something through with a sounding board

When you're about to communicate with your partner, it's helpful to compare notes on what you're each hoping for from the conversation and whether those things are compatible. They can say what they're hoping from you, and you can then say whether that's something you have to offer, and vice versa. This may sound phoney or like hard work, but it really can be useful, especially when it's a tough conversation.

Conclusions

Like the love languages that we covered in Chapter 1, we've seen that people have very different preferences for how they like to communicate on a daily basis, and how they tackle the disagreements which arise between them.

Leona gave a particularly powerful example of a time when her partner went into practical mode after her father's funeral in order to distract himself from the painful situation, whereas she'd really been looking for a comforting conversation. This clearly demonstrates how important it is to be able to make sense of our partner's seemingly strange behaviours for enduring love!

'I had tears streaming down my face and I was obviously in a bit of a mess. He looked across to a garage we were driving past. He pulled in and said, "I'm just gonna go and have a quick look"! And he got out of the car and went and had a look at the BMWs and the Mercedes that were over there. And then he got back in and carried on driving. I was mad with him but I just couldn't get anything out! He didn't see anything wrong with doing that. That's just the way he handles it as opposed to the way that I handle it.'

Like many of the people we've met in this chapter, Leona has realised that she and her partner handle these kinds of situations in different ways. Such understanding is a big part of why their relationship has lasted over time, as well as why she can laugh about the experience in retrospect. She recognised that to get the support that she needed to work through her grief, she had to lean on a friend outside the relationship.

In Chapter 5, we explore the crucial role of these kinds of 'significant others' in our relationships. Before that, in the next chapter, we'll turn to something that could be seen as a specific form of communication – sex and other forms of physical intimacy.

SUMMARY SUGGESTIONS: IT'S NOT WHAT YOU SAY...

Here are a few more things to try yourself, based on this chapter.

- Make some time with a partner or friend to find out an aspect of them that you don't already know about. You probably don't need 36 questions, you could just both think of an area of each other's history or opinions that you've never really talked about, and come prepared with a few questions about that.
- Think about something that you both find funny, such as a particular TV series, stand-up comedian, or silly activity. Make time to do that together. Or just have a conversation about what makes you laugh.
- Spend some time together in silence. You could go for a walk and sit quietly somewhere pleasant. Try not talking for a while, or even sit together looking at each other but not speaking. What's that like for you both?
- Try a kind of communication that you don't usually do in your relationship, for example having an Internet chat or a phone/Skype conversation or sending each other letters.
- Remember a recent argument and imagine what it might have felt like from the other person's perspective. Try writing down how it was for you first, and then how you think it might've been from their point of view.
- Have a meta-communication conversation. Find out what kinds of communication you each find easiest and which you find most difficult. What do you have in common and what do you differ on?

CHAPTER 4
LET'S TALK ABOUT SEX

Couples who rarely or never have sex
can know lifelong love

– bell hooks

You might wonder why we've left it so long in the book to get around to sex. We hear a lot in the media about how important sex is for relationships. Sex is seen as so vital that when we talk about people being 'in a relationship' we generally mean they're having sex with each other. 'Experts' say it's important for partners to have regular 'great sex' and that not doing so is a 'bad sign' for their relationship.

But think back to Chapter 3 when we considered the things that people like best about their relationships. Sex was nowhere on that list. People prioritise other kinds of closeness and contact much more highly than they do sex, with shared laughter featuring far more often than shared orgasms. Similarly, as we saw in Chapter 1, people generally feel more appreciated when their partner brings them a cup of tea in bed than when they initiate a raunchy encounter.

This isn't to say that our research found that sex wasn't *at all* important in relationships, rather it simply wasn't *as essential* as you might expect from all the hype. As with everything else we've covered in this book, diversity is the rule. Sex is a vital part of a relationship for some people. For others it's enjoyable but not crucial – something they can take or leave. And for some it isn't a feature of their relationship at all. Also it's very clear that the importance of sex is something that changes over time.

Many partners feel it's important to have some kind of physical intimacy, but it doesn't have to be sexual. This raises questions about where we draw the line between sex and other kinds of closeness. Our research suggests that it can be difficult when there's a big discrepancy in desire between partners – if one wants a lot more physical intimacy than the other, or a different kind of intimacy, for example. You might remember from Chapter 3 that a discrepancy in sexual desire is among the top ten things that people like least about their relationships. But such differences don't mean that people aren't happy with their relationship in other ways. In this chapter we'll suggest how you can navigate the fluctuations that happen in physical intimacy over time and the discrepancies there'll inevitably be between you in the type and amount of physical intimacy that you prefer.

Is sex that important?

Alongside the *Enduring Love?* study we've also been involved with another big research project over the last couple of years: a study of sex advice. We looked at all the bestselling sex manuals, along with newspaper and magazine problem pages, websites and TV advice programmes about sex. One thing that nearly all of this sex advice says is that sex is essential. Sex advisors even claim that it's a 'basic human need', like eating or breathing, and that it's good for your health.

Even more than that, sex advice generally claims that sex is vital for relationships. Most authors say that sex is the 'glue' that holds relationships together and that it's 'critical for marital health'. Books, magazines and TV programmes encourage people to 'keep their relationship alive' by learning different sexual techniques and positions to 'spice up' their sex life. They warn against having a 'sexless' relationship as if this would be the worst thing imaginable and would inevitably lead to your relationship falling apart.

So the sense from sex advice is that everybody should be having a consistent amount of sex and that it isn't okay for this to diminish over time. Also, partners should want the same kinds of sex as each other and at the same frequency. Any discrepancy between them is seen as a problem to be solved.

These messages about sex are absolutely wrong. More than that, they can also be really damaging if people take them seriously. Before we go on to say why, think about whether you've heard any of these ideas yourself, and whether you believe them.

What do we actually know about sex?

As you'll see in a moment, these common ideas about sex definitely don't fit with what we found in our research. They also don't fit with bigger sex surveys that other researchers carried out around the same time as we did our project.

The National Survey of Sexual Attitudes and Lifestyles (NATSAL) is a major sex survey which happens every ten years in Britain. In 2013 the survey found that over the past two decades the amount of sex that people have has actually gone down. The average number of times per month that people aged 16–44 have sex has decreased from five to three since the early 1990s. So people are having sex on average less than once a week. Also there's a massive variation around that average, with some people having no sex or very little sex and others having lots. Despite this, the majority of people (around two-thirds) still said that they were satisfied with their sex lives. So having lots of sex clearly isn't vital to everyone.

The NATSAL study also found that 42 per cent of men and 51 per cent of women reported one or more sexual difficulties. So it certainly isn't 'normal' for people to be having lots of unproblematic 'great sex', no matter what you might be led to believe by magazines and Hollywood movies. From these statistics it seems like it's actually *more* common to be struggling with sex to some degree than it is to have no sexual problems.

Finally, the NATSAL survey found that while sex was certainly an important part of a relationship for many people, having less sex or having a sexual problem wasn't linked to being dissatisfied with your relationship. The idea that sex is essential for healthy and happy relationships just isn't borne out by the data.

Think about where you fit in relation to the NATSAL study. Would you say you're satisfied with your sex life? Is how you feel about your sex life linked to how satisfied you are with your relationship more broadly or not? How do you feel about the amount of sex you have? Is sex something that you struggle with? If so, remember that means you're actually quite normal!

Another important new area of sex research is research on asexuality. In the last decade or so there's been a huge growth in asexual communities, that is, groups of people who don't experience sexual attraction. With increasing Internet access, asexual people have been able to find each other and to build communities of support. The AVEN website is a good place to find out more about this if you're interested.

Contrary to popular belief, there's absolutely nothing unhealthy about not wanting sex. Asexual people have no more psychological problems than anybody else. There's also a lot of diversity within asexuality. Some asexual people hate the idea of sex while others are neutral about it and might sometimes be sexual in order to give a partner pleasure. Some have occasional sexual feelings – for example, on their own or with a particular person – others have none at all. Some people have always been asexual; others experience periods of asexuality at certain times in their lives.

Asexual people give us a clue to an important fact about sex which doesn't come across in most sex manuals: sexual desire is on a spectrum just like so many other things about human beings, such as height, hair colour, or musical ability. Again, diversity is the rule. Sex is a high priority in some relationships and not important at all in others – and everything else between those two extremes. Many people vary over time with periods of higher or lower libido across their lives; others stay in the same place with their level of sexual desire remaining pretty constant.

From all of these studies we can see that sex is neither a fundamental human need nor is it essential to relationships. People have different levels and different types of sexual desire. So it's worth being very sceptical indeed of sex advice which puts forward a one-size-fits-all approach.

Pause for a moment to think about whether your own level of sexual attraction and desire has varied over time or not. On reflection, do you think that it's generally high or low? Can you accept that 'it is what it is' rather than wishing it was different? That's often quite difficult because of all the pressure we're under about sex.

Putting sex in its place

Our own research agreed wholeheartedly with the findings of the NATSAL study and research on asexuality. While the majority of people did appreciate some form of physical intimacy in their relationships, they varied hugely over whether it was important for that intimacy to be sexual or not. For example, when they looked through a set of photographs showing different forms of physical affection, Linda and James identified much more with people cuddled up on a settee than with any of the more sexual photos.

> 'That's more us in the sofa together, or on a park bench together, or having a coffee together. It's not that we don't do anything together, it's just not sex.'

We'll talk more about the different forms that physical intimacy can take shortly. In the meantime it's worth noting that even for those who *did* regard sex as important this didn't lessen the value they gave to other forms of intimacy and closeness in their relationship.

For example, Zoe agreed with the common sex advice idea that sex cemented her relationship, but she also prioritised other things as equally vital:

'That physical part of our relationship has always been really, really important. It's the glue that holds you together. It's an essential part of who we are together and what drew us to be together and sustained us over the years as well.'

'But the key thing as far as I see it is we're just incredibly good friends. I mean we're lovers as well and partners. We just really like each other and enjoy each other's company and have lots of shared humour and shared love of music and theatre and arts and things. It's just an incredible kind of privilege to be with someone who you love that much.'

It seems that for Zoe and her partner, friendship, shared interests and humour were certainly at least as important as sex in bonding them together and sustaining their relationship. Rose and Hugh made a similar point, going so far as to say that other things were far *more* vital for them to put energy into.

Rose: Sex is one of the prerequisites of a relationship for me, and I think for you. But there are other areas of a relationship that I think need a lot more work, and are far more important, like trust, money, love, teamwork.
Hugh: There are things that are more enduring.

These kinds of ideas were echoed by many people. They saw sex as one thing among many in their relationship mix. This doesn't diminish the significance of sex but it does put it into perspective. For example, we loved the way that Alun and Eleri put sex in its place when they spoke about the other, unique-to-them, kinds of physical contact that they appreciated.

Alun: Ooh. Sexual intercourse.
Eleri: Okay, well we do it!

Alun: Yes, we have sex.

Eleri: It's not just about sex, though, is it?

Alun: Affection.

Eleri: Intimacy.

Alun: Intimacy. We're quite tactile, aren't we? We're quite huggy, kissy, touchy and feely.

Eleri: Yes sometimes we hold hands brushing our teeth! I hadn't noticed it before and it's ridiculous! Holding hands: it's impractical! We've got a tiny bathroom and we have to shove each other out of the way to spit!

Lots of people, like Alun and Eleri, focused on ordinary, everyday kinds of intimacy like this. Indeed, returning to where we started this book, some who prioritised 'hot sex' in their relationship put it on level-pegging with cups of tea!

'Hot sex and cups of tea... great combination!'

Making space for intimacy

In Chapter 1 you saw that 'physical affection' was one of the top five answers people gave to the question of what their partner did to make them feel appreciated. But what exactly did they mean by that? Before we consider the kinds of physical intimacy that people prefer, think about which kinds are important to you. Do you like touching and/or being touched, and if so, in what ways? Which intimacy could you live without and which feels essential to you?

Physical intimacy

When it comes to physical contact, people particularly seem to like hugs and cuddles, kisses, stroking, and massage.

'Hugs and kisses.'

'Rubs my back every night.'

People didn't always make it clear whether these things were fleeting gestures or more extended moments of intimacy. Was it a kiss on the way out of the door or a long smooch on the sofa? A quick stroke of the back or a full-on massage? Probably the answer to this would be different for different relationships. However, people did often say that they appreciated physical affection being a regular thing rather than a one-off. For example:

'Greets me with a kiss every evening when I come in from work.'

'He gives me a foot rub every evening.'

One couple, Oscar and Manuel, reflected that being in physical contact was a kind of default situation for them whenever they were sitting together, even as we were interviewing them.

Oscar: If we watch something together, I think we're usually cuddling. Not very aggressively cuddling! But just touching each other.
Manuel: Well, we are now!

As with all the other forms of appreciation that we covered in Chapter 1 a key point here is that the kind of physical affection which people prefer is unique to them. You can't just transfer it from one relationship to another. This is another problem with sex advice, which tends to claim that the same sexual technique or position will be good for everybody. For example, having your arm stroked can be unbearably tickly for one person whereas another person finds it soothing and gentle, another finds it a little too rough, and another finds it erotic. It can also feel different on different occasions depending on how tired or turned-on a person is. As you saw with communication in the last chapter, preferences vary wildly and it's important to know where your partner is coming from rather than expecting – for example – that they'll like to be touched in the same way that your ex-partner did. It's good to anticipate that people will have different preferences and not to make assumptions or imply that somebody *should* enjoy a specific activity.

As with other forms of communication, styles of physical affection can be something that you learn growing up. Rodney spoke about this:

'I think it's in my nature. I'm a tactile person. I think I have that from my father. And my partner's family also is very huggy. We both come from families where you express affection, physically, by big hugs and holding hands and stuff like that.'

It's also worth remembering that giving the same kind of physical affection to a partner that you'd like for yourself can easily backfire. Like the love languages that we explored in Chapter 1, what works for you may well not work for them. It's useful to show them what you'd like, but not to assume that they'll like the same thing.

Also, we don't always have it in us to provide the kind of physical intimacy that our partner might like most. Here Lucy and Garry grapple with this issue around massages.

Lucy: I would love a massage.

Garry: Sometimes Lucy says, 'can you massage my feet please?' and I'll say, 'yes, okay.'

Lucy: There's no joy in it for him.

Garry: So I'll start massaging Lucy's feet and then I'll say, 'oh, my hands are getting tired.'

Lucy: Within about three seconds.

Garry: Three seconds! No!

Lucy: You see this hedge around the house? It's about 70 foot long or something. This is the man that can cut that entire hedge and take the whole day to do it. It's a big job. He is a strong, fit man. Apart from when it comes to massage. He can put his hands on my shoulders and then, 'ooh... that's just too much like hard work.'

Garry: But, at other times, like when you were pregnant and when you've not been well I have done a proper job.

In this kind of situation it's worth thinking about whether you can offer a person's second- or third-favourite form of physical affection rather than making a half-hearted attempt at something that you clearly aren't enjoying!

Not all partners draw a clear dividing line between physical intimacy and other forms of intimacy. Sitting close together, gesturing at each other across a crowded room, and gazing into each other's eyes, are all forms of intimacy – they just don't involve actual touching. For Brendan and Josh, for example, what seemed important was sharing something or being alongside each other: it wasn't necessarily about physical contact.

Brendan: Intimacy can also be having a cup of tea together: making a pot for two, that's nice. Or sitting and reading. You don't have to make an effort to talk to each other or need to be sitting up straight and looking your best for each other. You can just relax.

Josh: Yes sharing something that's happening, or just being next to each other when we're both doing our own thing.

TOP TIP

With a partner, or somebody else that you share a physical connection with, each make a list of your top five kinds of non-sexual physical intimacy, or affection that doesn't involve physical contact.

Make a time over the next week to experience one thing on your list and one thing on theirs that you both fancy. Try to let go of any assumptions. Let them show and tell you exactly how they like it, and vice versa, and give yourself some time to enjoy it.

Public displays of affection

One form of physical contact which partners often have very different feelings about is the public display of affection or PDA. Eleri and Alun both enjoy these but they have a different sense of where they'd put themselves on a scale from 'acceptable' PDAs to 'get a room!'

> **Eleri:** If we're affectionate in public we're a bit icky about it. Other people say 'get a room'.
> **Alun:** But we do it quite a lot.
> **Eleri:** We don't snog or anything like that in public.
> **Alun:** Yes we do, we do!
> **Eleri:** I didn't think we did!
> **Alun:** Yes we do.

Other partners, like Arundhati and Anish, were clear that PDAs just weren't a part of their relationship. They were comfortable being physically affectionate in private, or in the dark at a movie theatre, but not in the park or any other kind of public context. The degree of comfort people feel can depend on cultural, class, or family background. Think about whether PDAs were something you saw growing up, or whether they were frowned upon or just didn't happen.

Octavia has learnt that PDAs just aren't an option for her partner. He isn't even happy holding hands or gazing at each other. This means that he has to introduce her as his partner before people know what their relationship is.

> *'Even if we walk in together nobody knows unless if he says "this is so and so". Sometimes I just stand there and look at him. He doesn't like that.'*

Octavia's example shows how PDAs, like other forms of touch, can have very different meanings for different people. It sounds like her partner is intensely uncomfortable about PDAs. Perhaps they make him feel trapped, or he worries about how people who don't have a happy relationship might feel if they see him and Octavia holding hands. For Octavia though, touching is a sign that her partner is proud of their relationship, giving her reassurance that he wants other people to know that they're together.

Long-term conflicts can easily bubble away between partners over the years if one person won't engage in the kind of physical touch that the other person wants. The conflict is often rooted in the assumption that it means the same thing for both people. For example, Lucy might feel like Garry just can't be bothered to do small things that would help her, like giving her a massage. But it may be that Garry just doesn't have a clue how to do it and feels clumsy and stupid when he tries – unlike cutting the hedge, which he knows he's good at. Octavia might feel rejected by her husband not wanting a PDA when actually it's about him wanting to appear professional in places where his work colleagues might be present, and nothing at all to do with his feelings for her.

PDAs also have different meanings in different contexts. Several same-sex partners who we spoke to said that they didn't hold hands or kiss in public because they feared abuse or discrimination. This was particularly true for younger people in same-sex relationships. For people in non-monogamous relationships, PDAs could similarly feel awkward or risky. Differences between partners in ethnicity or age can also mean negative reactions when they're public in their affection.

Alternatively, some of us find it empowering to make PDAs in these kinds of circumstances, to show the world that we're proud of our relationships. It's worth remember that PDAs for these groups of people involves making a decision about whether to be 'out' or not, which makes it a much more emotionally loaded decision. Again, partners in a relationship can have different views on this, which can be tough to navigate. Some of the advice about communicating in Chapter 3 might be helpful if that's the case for you.

Think about where you stand on PDAs on the spectrum from wanting them all of the time to finding them terrifying or cringeworthy. Are there some places where they feel comfortable for you and others less so? Are you more comfortable with them from some people than from others? What do they mean to you? Have you shared opinions around PDAs with past or current partners or not?

Sleeping together

One type of physical closeness that's important for many people is contact before or during sleep. People say that they particularly appreciate things like the following:

'We often hold hands as we're going to sleep.'

'Strokes my hair until I sleep.'

'Snuggles up to me in the night.'

For Emma and Jake it's important that they always go up to bed at the same time, even if they fall asleep at different times. This is *the* moment in the day when they can share some physical closeness. Emma said:

'Sometimes I'll fall asleep if we're watching something: I'll fall asleep earlier. Sometimes, particularly at weekends, he falls asleep. But then we'll always go up to bed together.'

For Georgina this kind of 'sleep-sync' goes as far as automatically knowing when she and her partner are ready for bed. Their bodies seem to be attuned to each other in this way:

'What I've noticed, and which made me feel very tickled, is that, when Anton rises to go and sleep, my system says that it's time to go to sleep. I could stay for a while, but my system is still telling me it's time now. Anton has gone so it's time to go. And also vice versa. When I'm very tired and then I get up it doesn't take five minutes and Anton comes.'

However, as we'll see shortly, by no means all partners share beds or sleep together every night. Some chose to have separate bedrooms or sleep separately because they live in different houses (see Chapter 2). Some have such different body rhythms or patterns to their working days that sleeping with each other just isn't an option. And some have other people sharing their beds some or all of the time. Think, for now, about your preferences around sleeping. Do you prefer to sleep together or separately? Or perhaps you like to vary it? Is it important to you to go to bed at the same time as a partner – or does this not matter for you?

Sexual intimacy

It's useful to question the dividing line that we often draw between sex and other forms of physical intimacy. For many people that line isn't so clear. For example, we've already seen that many people put these two things on an equal footing rather than prioritising sex. For example, saying that they appreciate: *'Intimacy, passion and sex.'* Or *'I love having sex and cuddling with my partner.'*

Leah made it clear that the space that she and Usha created in their relationship for physical contact was the important thing for them. It might become sexual but that wasn't the reason why they cuddled up together.

'If we're cuddling then the cuddle will sometimes turn into sexual intimacy.'

Similarly, Anne and Henry emphasised closeness over sex, making time for lying down together with no pressure for it to go in any particular direction.

Henry: I really like our cuddles or something where we just go to the bed and lie on the bed together and hug.
Anne: Yes, kisses.

Henry: Not particularly sexual, but just being very, very close, and feeling our bodies next to each other. I think it's very bodily, but it's not necessarily sexual, it's just about being close and very comfortable with each other.

Anne: Yes, I might touch your tummy or something like that!

Henry: Yes, it's nice.

Interestingly both these couples have hit upon something that sex therapists recommend. That is that partners make time for physical closeness with absolutely no pressure for it to become sexual. Therapists suggest the 'sensate focus' technique for people who're having sexual difficulties. This involves taking sex off the menu entirely and just focusing on learning how each person likes to touch and be touched. Some people then gradually build sex back into their time together, while others find they're happy with other forms of physical affection.

This all brings us to the question of what we even *mean* by sex. At what point do Leah and Usha decide that a cuddle has become sexual, and why don't Anne and Henry class tummy-touching as sex? It might seem like an obvious question, but really it isn't. For example, some people assume that sex is something that involves a penis entering a vagina but none of the same-sex partners in our research have sex that way, and some of the male–female partners don't either. Similarly, sex certainly doesn't always involve orgasms. Orgasms are a crucial part of sex for some people but others don't need that kind of climax, or they enjoy giving orgasms more than they do getting them. After the popularity of the *Fifty Shades of Grey* books and movies people have become more aware of the diversity of types of sensation and role-play that some people experience as sexual and pleasurable, whereas others would have no interest in that kind of thing at all.

We can ask ourselves when physical intimacy becomes sexual intimacy, when tactile becomes sensual, or when sensual becomes sexual, but that might be missing the point. Perhaps these lines that we draw don't matter anywhere near as much as figuring out the kinds of touch that we enjoy – and don't enjoy – and communicating this to our partners. We'll come back to some suggestions about how to do this towards the end of the chapter. For now try this quiz.

QUIZ TIME: HOW IMPORTANT ARE DIFFERENT KINDS OF PHYSICAL INTIMACY?

This is a list of some of the different kinds of physical intimacy that came up in our study. Go through and tick the ones that are important to you and put a cross next to the ones you really don't like. You could even rate them on a scale of 1–10 on how important they are, or give letters to indicate whether you enjoy giving them (G) or receiving them (R). You can add your own ones of course, to extend the list if you want to.

Cuddles	Holding hands walking	Bondage
Hair stroking	Penetrative sex	A quick hug
Snogging/ smooching	Curling up by TV	Kissing in public
Oral sex	Tickling	Sleeping together
Manual sex	Back massage	Spanking
Light kisses	Arm stroking	Hand-holding at home
Back scratching	Knee/leg stroking	Snuggling up asleep
Foot rub	Kissing all over	Shower together
Love bites	Ear lobe nibbling	Shoulder rub
Sensual massage	Bathing together	Anal stimulation
Using sex toys	Feather stroking	Sexy role-play
Stroking chest/ breasts	Bear hugs	Head massage
Food–sex play	Masturbating together	Sex fully clothed (dry-humping)

Intimacy and parenting

You might have got the idea so far in this chapter that people are completely free to find the kinds of physical intimacy that suit their relationship. Please don't go away with that impression! For one thing, it's clear that all the pressure from sex advice and other media means that most people don't *feel* free at all. They actually spend a great deal of time and energy trying to conform to what they think a 'normal' or 'great' sex life looks like, even if they don't enjoy it remotely.

Also the realities of many people's lives often mean that they're not free to figure out what they enjoy most, or to engage with their partner in that way. One major finding from our research, for example, was that people with children felt more dissatisfied than others about how often they had sex or physical intimacy.

Generally speaking, for male–female couples, fathers wanted sex more often than mothers did, although for some couples it was the other way around. Fathers were more than twice as likely as mothers to say that discrepancy in their sexual desire was the thing that they like least about their relationship. Mothers often said that they wanted to have sex less often than their partner did:

'We don't have sex very often (small children) and we don't talk about this.'

'Our sex life is not great since having children.'

However, although people didn't like these discrepancies in sexual desire, they tended to see them as part and parcel of parenting and the discrepancy didn't impact on how satisfied they were with their relationship as a whole.

Ken and Sue said that parenting was the reason why their focus had shifted from sex to other kinds of physical affection:

Sue: Once children come along that all gets a little bit harder.
Ken: That all goes out the window!

Sue: A little bit harder to do that now.

Ken: But sitting on the settee together, we do that and things like that.

Sue: Yes a lot.

Other parents spoke in more detail about the reasons for sex 'going out the window'. There were lots of different reasons but, for many, it was because one or both parents were too tired after juggling work, domestic chores, and childcare. For some, especially mothers, the struggle to shift from being a parent to being a sexual being again was also hard work – emotionally and practically.

Young parents, Daniela and Darren, spoke about how the sexual side of their relationship had changed since their children came along. Their experience links back to what we covered in Chapter 2 about the importance of space in the home, because it was the fact that they no longer had a room to themselves which had the biggest impact.

Daniela: It would be so nice to have our own room again because even when we're in there talking to each other we have to be careful we're not going to wake them up. Sometimes I suppose you could feel like you're not a proper couple, because we're sharing a room with two young kids, and we can't have our own space. It's one of those things.

Darren: It is, just something you can't really get round.

Daniela: It doesn't make it any easier when we want to be on our own. Especially at the moment: our baby's obviously in the bedroom, I'm breastfeeding. But that's not going to be forever, either. I think if we had a bit more privacy, there would be more closeness, because that's the way we always have been in our relationship.

Darren: Yes. I think we've both just come to accept it as it is, so far.

Like many people, Darren and Daniela saw the decrease in the sexual side of their relationship as an inevitable part of becoming parents. But you can also see that it was tough for them because it made them feel like they weren't a 'proper couple'.

It's very important to realise that having less sex, or no sex at all, doesn't mean that a relationship is somehow inferior. Parenting often alters the kind of physical intimacy that happens in relationships. It may be that the sexual dynamic of a relationship changes temporarily, or irreversibly, before and after having children. What's important is finding ways of making this 'new' relationship work for you.

If you have children yourself, think on whether this impacted on your sex life, and – if so – in what ways? What are your feelings about this? We'll come to some suggestions about what you can do about such fluctuations shortly.

Bed-time

Historically, sleeping arrangements have varied a lot. In some communities people generally have their own bedrooms, and in many cultures parents, children and extended family share a bed. Neither sleeping apart nor sleeping with children should be a cause of shame. As with everything we've covered in this book, the message is that different people do it in different ways – and that's okay. Whatever works for you and your relationship is fine.

Even so, one of the main reasons that parents give for changes in physical intimacy is the ways in which their sleeping arrangements change when children come along. Even parents whose houses had room for separate children's bedrooms found that the arrival of babies changed where and how they slept.

Garry: We play musical beds at times, don't we?
Lucy: Yes we do.

Garry: A normal night, I would say, is me up in the attic, Lucy and Alex together, and Lois in her room.

Many people in our research recognised themselves in this picture!

Linda: Many people in the bed.
James: Oh yes that's us there. Yes and the cat comes as well.

One older Gujarati couple spoke about bed-sharing as part of their culture – it was something that connected them through the generations. In their emotion maps grandparents and grandchildren were routinely shown sharing a bed. This reminds us that not everybody prefers separate space, despite this being a Western cultural norm.

Another person, Nelushi, talked about bed-sharing on trips home to India as a scene of jubilation and a way of consolidating a sense of extended-family togetherness.

'When I go back home and live with my parents we don't sleep in our own rooms, we sleep together in the same room. My mother's got a huge bed so my father and the children and everybody else is in the same bed and then we have sleeping bags on the carpet around them. My sister has a little baby as well, so there's my father, my mother, myself, my two children, my sister and her child all in one room. And the children are noisy, jumping, dancing till late in the night. Everybody's laughing and talking and then we all sleep together.'

Other people use bed-sharing to keep boundaries between the generations. Magdalena, for example, only allows it at the weekends:

'My daughter likes to just spend the weekend with me. She would like to sleep with me and all the kids, so we just gather together and just have a weekend together, and then weekdays they go back to their beds.'

Sue and Ken's children are only allowed to join their parents in bed in the mornings. However they admitted that these rules were harder to enforce with the family cat!

Sue: They would come in in the mornings: that was all.
Ken: Yes we would never have them sleeping all night with us.
Sue: We were quite strict about them being in their own beds.
Ken: Yes because they get used to it otherwise. But the cat does!
Sue: Yes the cat's a nuisance now.

Manuel and Oscar reminded us that children could have a lasting impact on parents' sleeping habits even after they've grown up and moved away!

Manuel: I didn't sleep well last night because I felt I always had to lie on my side so as not to fall out of bed. We talk about maybe moving in together in autumn or so, and then we would have our own bed which would be much wider so that we can sleep comfortably in it.

Oscar: It depends on Daniel's university plans.

For others, it's not just the arrival of children that shifts sleeping patterns, but also changes in health. Ted commented on how he and Alan had changed their sleeping arrangements after a period of illness and these patterns then simply stuck:

'We did sleep in the same bed for some time but then agreed I would go into the smaller bedroom because we were more comfortable. We could roll about at our own will and so on. I could get up if I wanted to. Alan could get up and do whatever. And we're perfectly happy with that.'

Like sex, sharing a bed is often seen as a part of a 'proper relationship', but this is another myth that's worth challenging. Actually, one in five of the people we surveyed said that they didn't always sleep together. And sleep research has found that people who sleep alone often sleep more soundly. So, for many partners, having the option of sleeping apart for at least some of the time can be beneficial, both personally and for the relationship.

It can be a big relief for people to find out that they're not out of the ordinary or 'doing it wrong' if they don't sleep together; just as it's a relief to find out that other people have less sex – or no sex – over time in their relationships.

Fluctuations and discrepancies

Hopefully, this chapter has convinced you that we need to think again about what makes a healthy and normal sex life. Instead of the one-size-fits-all model of sex manuals, we need to understand that – like so many aspects of relationships

– different things work for different people, and things change over the course of our lives. Any level of desire, or type of physical intimacy, can be healthy, so long as everybody involved is in agreement.

Fluctuation in sexual desire over time is inevitable, as is some discrepancy between partners in what kinds of physical intimacy they prefer and how often. Instead of viewing these things as problems to be solved, changes and differences in sexual desire can be *expected* and *accepted*.

Fluctuations over time

You've already seen how people who become parents experience changes in their levels of desire and how this can impact on the kinds of physical contact they have. But it's not just parenting that causes these kinds of shifts over the course of a relationship. Our bodies change over time in ways that mean we may well want less, or more, physical intimacy. Also the levels of desire that we have and what we find exciting can change a lot over time.

Human sexuality is rarely completely static. For some people it may just be that they notice a small decrease or increase in how much sex they want, or changes in their sexual fantasies, or what kinds of touch they prefer. For others, it can be a complete change in the kind of people they find attractive or whether they want to have sex at all.

Everyone who'd been together for several years spoke about shifts and changes in physical intimacy during their relationship. For example, Janet and Robert commented on a picture we showed them of a young couple kissing in the bath.

Janet: Certainly have done that but we don't do it now.
Robert: No.
Janet: I think the dynamics do change.

Body changes have an impact on the kinds of physical intimacy that are possible. While Ted, who we met earlier, was happy with the change in sleeping arrangements following his illness, he was less happy that it had left him unable to get erections because that meant that he and Alan couldn't share the same kinds of sex that they'd previously enjoyed.

The ability to 'perform' sexually is often seen by wider society as a vital part of masculinity. So, however supportive a partner may be, loss of erections can take a major toll. Again it can be very helpful to broaden out the definition of what 'counts' as sex or intimacy here: to build in time for closeness without pressure for it to be sexual, and/or to have the kinds of sex that don't require an erection.

Many partners found that humour was important in dealing with changes that happened in their sex lives over time. For example, Clive said:

> 'You can find a comedy element creep in because you're trying to be intimate but you're having a battle with the bedclothes, which is like "there's three of us in this relationship – me, you and the duvet!" We might as well give up! And you can have that laugh because there isn't the pressure of "we must have it now"'.

For Clive and his partner, making a joke and sharing a laugh together helped to alleviate pressures around sexual performance. They found that their relationship was all the stronger because of the different kinds of closeness that developed as a result of changes in their sex lives.

Another couple, Martin and Margaret, had also experienced fluctuations in their sex life. In this case it was Margaret who was now less interested in sex. Like men, women can feel pressure to remain sexual, often because of the cultural pressures on women to be sexually desirable. This can mean that some women feel they have to keep on having sex even if they don't want it. Again, in Margaret and Martin's case laughter helped them to work through this period of their lives. Talking about it with openness and affectionate banter, they steered a path between having as much sex as Martin might want, and no sex at all.

> **Margaret:** The sex-starved marriage. Oh you can relate to that, poor Martin, after my hormones packed up.
>
> **Martin:** We had one or two books that we were looking at.
>
> **Margaret:** But sex is so painful now that it isn't adventurous any more.
>
> **Martin:** You tend to sort of do it for my benefit rather than for yourself, don't you? But you seem to enjoy it. You're good at conning me if you're not.
>
> **Margaret:** Well, I make the best of it, shall I say. We've got a lot of intimacy. You're not sex starved, but slightly sex hungry at times. We have a joke as well, don't we? We laugh. So instead of being passionate it is quite entertaining!

As we saw in Chapter 3, the ability to laugh together, even about potentially painful and embarrassing things like this, really does seem to be a vital form of relationship glue, more important than sex itself.

Of course, different people respond to problems in different ways. For example, other people in Martin and Margaret's situation might navigate such changes in different ways: stopping having sex, focusing on other forms of intimacy, finding forms of sex that aren't painful – manual or oral sex, for example – or using lubricants or introducing sex toys into their sexual repertoire. Again, a degree of humour and playfulness can be helpful for navigating these changes and bringing in different ideas.

In addition to ageing, and simply being together for a long time, sex also tends to change after a difficult life event, such as the death of a parent, a miscarriage, physical or mental health problems, or losing a job. We'll come back to these kinds of things in the last chapter of the book but it's worth remembering here that such events are another reason why sex will definitely fluctuate over time, and that's okay.

We also shouldn't assume that sex will always *decline* as people get older or remain in a long-term relationship. Our research showed that changes over time were also often in the other direction. Some couples, for example, found that they were having a lot *more* sex now that they were older because they weren't working so hard and they weren't tired all the time. Some parents' relationships had a 'second life' once their children had left home.

Maturing and getting to know each other more deeply can also help to enrich a couple's sex life. For some, deepening intimacy meant that they had sex less often but that it was more fulfilling when it did happen. For one couple, finding ways to bring newness or a sense of adventure into their sex life brought risqué pleasures that were mutually exciting.

> 'We occasionally meet with an escort, to help maintain an exciting and maybe risqué secret life. Very consenting and fully enjoyed by us both.'

The important thing to remember here, as always, is that different things work for different people. Like this couple you might like the idea of occasionally 'spicing up' your sex life – as recommended by sex manuals. Or this might not be for you at all. You might find that sex becomes more or less frequent over time, or more or less fulfilling. It may well change many times over the course of a long relationship. Expecting and accepting changes can be more helpful than trying to desperately hold on to the same type and frequency of physical intimacy.

Think back over your own life so far. Have there been times when you wanted sex more, or less? Have the kinds of things you fantasised about and/or found erotic changed over time? How have you navigated these things in your relationships?

Discrepancies between partners

Fluctuations in desire over time are probably easiest to manage if they affect each person in similar ways. If two people in a relationship both find that they want less sex over time there's very little problem, apart from any social pressure they might feel to have sex in order to be a 'proper couple'.

However, it's pretty inevitable that there'll be times in any long-term relationship when there's some discrepancy between partners, either in the amount of physical intimacy that they want, or in the type of desires that they have. The NATSAL survey found that, at any point in time, at least one in four people in relationships didn't share the same level of interest in sex as their partner.

While we were doing our research, a story hit the headlines which highlighted just how difficult this can be for people. A husband was so unhappy about the amount of sex in his marriage that he kept a daily spreadsheet for a month of his wife's responses to his requests for sex. The spreadsheet noted whether sex occurred and, if not, what his wife's 'excuse' was. According to the spreadsheet, sex happened on three occasions which, if you remember the NATSAL study, is actually around the national average. The wife's 'excuses' for not having sex included: feeling tired or sick, having to get up early the next day, having eaten too much, feeling 'gross' and needing a shower, wanting to finish watching something on TV, and 'non-verbal'. The husband gave the spreadsheet to his wife just as she was heading off on a ten-day business trip. She proceeded to post it to a relationships forum on the social-networking site Reddit. The post resulted in hundreds of comments, most taking sides with either the husband or the wife. Needless to say neither of their ways of handling things are remotely helpful in this kind of situation!

We did hear stories of similar conflicts about sex discrepancies in our research although fortunately they weren't played out in quite such a passive-aggressive or public way as the Reddit example! For instance, you might remember Peter, who we mentioned in Chapter 3, and how his partner struggled with the fact that he wanted to look at pornography online whereas she definitely didn't. Also Luke complained that his partner Louise only wanted sex 'every blue moon' and that, like the wife in the Reddit case, she often engineered things so that sex couldn't happen – for example with the rule that she'd only have sex if she'd had a bath and was in bed by 10 p.m., which hardly ever happened.

VITAL STATISTICS:

who has the largest sex discrepancy?

Our research did find that the kind of gender dynamic in the Reddit example played out in a lot of male–female relationships. We heard several examples like those of Peter and Luke wanting more or different kinds of sex to their female partners. Also we found that women were generally much more likely than men to say that their partner wanted to have more sex than they did. Men were three times more likely than women to mention sexual intimacy as something that made them feel appreciated in their relationship. These gender differences were particularly marked with parents, compared with partners who didn't have children.

There was also more of a sex discrepancy in relationships that had been going for a long time compared with newer relationships. For partners who were going out together, or who lived apart (see Chapter 2), differences in desire were less than for those who lived together.

People in same-sex relationships tended to share levels of desire more than those in male–female relationships. This seems to support the idea that divergence in desire is often related to gender.

One reason for the gender difference in sexual discrepancies could be that women and men receive different messages about sex. For example, many women in our study valued sex when they felt desired by their partner and when their partner was generous and attentive.

'Very selfless and considerate during sex.'

'He is an incredibly generous lover.'

In contrast, many men valued sex when their own desires were fulfilled or – worryingly – even when a partner had sex despite not feeling turned-on themselves. This is something we'll come back to shortly when we consider the importance of consent.

'Indulges my sex fantasies.'

'Has sex when she doesn't really want to.'

So it could be partly that, at least in some relationships, women and men are looking for different things from sex. Another reason for discrepancies in desire may also relate back to the gender differences in domestic labour, which we've touched on in previous chapters.

Louise certainly acknowledged the role of underlying resentment in her diminished sex life with Luke. She said that sex had become increasingly unequal since they'd had children and she was now doing paid work all day *and* shouldering the bulk of the domestic labour and childcare. She and Luke both felt that there was an element of power in their patterns of sexual behaviour. Louise felt powerless against the unequal demands that were being placed on her. The one place where she *could* wield some power was the sexual side of their relationship. Perhaps withdrawing from sex was her way of communicating to Luke what it feels like when things become very unequal. At times when the children were being looked after by other relatives they noticed a shift in this dynamic and they both enjoyed sex, and time together more generally, a good deal more.

There's no one universal reason for gender differences in sexual desire, rather there are many different reasons which play out in different ways in different relationships. Social pressures around masculinity and femininity have a role, as do everyday life-circumstances like work and kids, but it's also important to remember that certainly not all relationships work out this way. In our research on sex advice we found that plenty of women write to agony columns complaining that they want *more* sex than their partners and plenty of men say that they don't really want sex much any more. Some women in our research also made it clear that they'd like more sex than they were getting:

'I'd like to have sex with him more frequently.'

'The thing I like least in our relationship: Lack of sex – not feeling like the centre of his universe.'

Think about how these kinds of discrepancies have played out in your own relationships. Have you found yourselves wanting different amounts of sex, or different types of sex, or both? How have you generally gone about tackling those kinds of differences? We'll now make some suggestions that you should find helpful with these kinds of fluctuations and discrepancies in future.

Navigating discrepancies

The most important thing about discrepancies in desire is that they should *never* be resolved by putting pressure on the person who doesn't want sex to have it anyway. Some – very dodgy – sex advice suggests that people should have sex when they don't want to in order to 'maintain their relationship', but this is just plain wrong. We've seen throughout this chapter that people can have perfectly happy, healthy, satisfying relationships when there's a sex discrepancy between them, or no sex at all in the relationship.

Pressurising somebody else – or yourself – to have sex that isn't really wanted is non-consensual sex. If the pressure is so high that somebody simply doesn't feel able to say 'no' then that's sexual abuse. If you get into the habit of having sex that one of you isn't really into, it's highly likely that the person who doesn't want it will feel less and less sexual over time. It makes the problem worse, not better. If you have sex with a partner when *you* don't really want to, without telling them, and they later find out, they may well be deeply upset and ashamed at the thought that they've unwittingly engaged in non-consensual sex.

Of course, as we've seen in this chapter, there are people like Margaret who're happy to meet their partner's sexual needs even when sex doesn't do much for them in terms of sexual pleasure. That's absolutely fine in situations where everybody knows what's going on, and when the person offering sex really doesn't feel under any pressure or coercion. Margaret, for example, may not have experienced sexual pleasure but she did experience pleasure in the intimacy of the moment.

It's up to the more sexual partner to ensure that their partner really *is* freely offering sex and finding some element of the experience pleasurable. Neither partner should be doing it, for example, because they fear losing the relationship or because they feel that a 'real man' or a 'real woman' should have sex. This is also why a one-size-fits-all model of sex is a bad idea. It tends to lead to some people doing things that they don't really want to do.

Try to get away from the idea that 'good', 'healthy' or 'normal' sex happens at a certain frequency or that it involves certain anatomy working in certain ways in certain positions. As we've seen, generally the most fulfilling sex – and physical intimacy – happens when you can be 'in the moment', just enjoying what you're doing, and not aiming at any particular goal. We find the following quote from the scholar Gayle Rubin to be a particularly useful reminder.

'Most people find it difficult to grasp that whatever they like to do sexually will be thoroughly repulsive to someone else, and that whatever repels them sexually will be the most treasured delight of someone, somewhere. Most people mistake their sexual preferences for a universal system that will or should work for everyone.'

This also helps us to remember to never make a partner feel bad about their sexual desires. Just because we don't share them doesn't mean there's anything wrong with having them – unless they try to pressure us into acting on them when we don't want to.

Sex is a massive topic, so we've included some suggestions in the final chapter of books that give advice about how to figure out what you like sexually and how to communicate about this with a partner. If you're not actually sure what you like sexually, then reading or watching erotica or porn can be helpful, as can reading collections of other people's sexual fantasies like Emily Dubberley's *Garden of Desires*. Alternatively try the following top tip.

TOP TIP

Make a 'yes, no, maybe' list – either alone or with a partner. Think up every single remotely sexual, erotic or sensual activity that you have ever heard of or can imagine. Write a long list of these down one side of a piece of paper.

Then go through the list writing 'yes', 'no' or 'maybe' for whether you'd like to do each item. Alternatively, you can score them or write notes, as with the physical intimacy quiz earlier. If you feel comfortable doing so, share the answers with a partner and talk through what turns you on and turns you off. Try and be as honest as possible – don't worry if the result is fits of giggles more than bouts of orgasm – after all, as you've seen in this chapter and the previous one, laughter is also an important part of intimacy!

There are also many versions of these available online, for example on the following web pages:

www.scarleteen.com/article/advice/yes_no_maybe_so_a_sexual_inventory_stocklist

www.bishuk.com/2015/03/08/omg-yes-not-for-me-hmmm-working-out-what-sex-you-want-to-have

www.charlieglickman.com/2010/03/12/yesnomaybe-lists

With sex discrepancies, some of the advice from Chapter 3 about communication is also useful: building empathy on both sides can really help. We've seen throughout this chapter that having sex, and not having sex, can mean different things for different people. So try to find out what sex means for your partner and then communicate what it means to you. For

TRY IT YOURSELF: SHARED AND SEPARATE DESIRES

If you're in a sexual relationship, fill in the following diagram together. If you're in a non-sexual relationship you could fill it in for other forms of physical intimacy. If you're not currently in a relationship you could think about which desires it would be important for you to share with a future partner, and which less so.

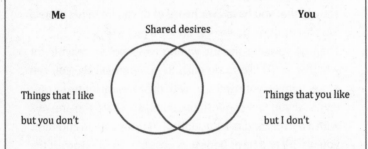

Me
You
Shared desires
Things that I like but you don't
Things that you like but I don't

An exercise like this can help spark a conversation about whether it's important for you to get some of your separate desires met and, if so, how you might do that within the context of your relationship rules. For example, could sexual fantasies, erotica, or pornography meet those needs or would that be a problem for you or your partner? We'll come back to these kinds of questions when we look more at relationship boundaries and monogamy in the next chapter.

example, compare the following meanings of sex that people told us they had:

'It makes me feel loved and cared for.'

'I love the release of orgasm: total stress relief.'

'Makes me feel I'm still attractive after all these years.'

'I feel confident and skilful when I can give my partner pleasure.'

Of course, sex may have more than one of these meanings – and many others – for each person. If there's a discrepancy in sexual desire in your relationship, it might be that you can find other ways to meet each other's needs besides sex. For example, different forms of physical contact can meet a need for closeness. Orgasms can be had alone as well as together. Dancing together may make some people feel attractive. The desire to feel confident and skilful in a relationship can be met by fixing things around the home or dealing with the finances rather than through sex.

Overall it's best to assume that there *will* be discrepancies in your sexual desires, just as in other aspects of your relationship. We saw in Chapter 1 how it can be helpful to map out the things you like to do together and separately. Here we've adapted that activity for sex.

Conclusions

We've seen throughout this chapter that sex and physical intimacy mean different things for different people: they can be positive features creating closeness and affection in relationships, or they can be ordinary and taken-for-granted, or they can become problematic and difficult. Sex can be everything, or nothing, or something in-between.

What *is* useful is to expect that there will be fluctuations in physical intimacy over time in your relationship and that there'll be some discrepancies in sexual desire between you in terms of what you want, how often you want it, and what it means to you.

SUMMARY SUGGESTIONS:
LET'S TALK ABOUT SEX

Based on this chapter, here are a few more things to try yourself.

- Consider how important – if at all – sex is to you. It's impossible to try to step outside of all the social messages we've received about sex, but try to be as honest with yourself as possible. What kinds of sex, if any, do you really enjoy? What is the meaning of sex for you? Which elements are important for you to have in a sexual experience? Which less so?
- Have some conversations with the people you're close to about what kind of physical contact you each like and don't like. Think about how you greet each other and say goodbye, for example. Do you shake hands, hug, or kiss? Is this the form of physical contact you'd both prefer? If not, can you negotiate a physical or non-physical greeting that would be more mutually enjoyable?
- Feeling sexy and wanting to be intimate is tough when you're tired, so explore your relationship with sleep. How important is sleep to you? Does it come easily or not? Do you like to doze or catnap? Do you like sleeping alone and/ or with a partner? Is sharing a bed something you chose to do or a necessity? What do you like to do in preparation for sleep? How do you like to wake up? Try to create your most preferred sleep situation at some time over the next month and really enjoy it.
- Write a paragraph description of the same sexual activity or physical contact that you've experienced as really fulfilling on one occasion and not so fulfilling at all on another. Compare your descriptions of the two times. What are the key things that make sex and/or intimacy fulfilling for you? Think about how you, and the person you're being intimate with, could help make sure those things are present.

CHAPTER 5
THE MAGIC NUMBER

One's life has value so long as one attributes value to the life of others, by means of love, friendship, and compassion
– Simone de Beauvoir

Over the last four chapters one key point that we've come back to is how different our relationships can be from others around us. Even though we didn't go out of our way to look for diversity, in our research that's exactly what we found. You've seen, for example, big differences in the kinds of 'us-time' and 'me-time' that people prefer; in their living situations; in how they communicate and express love; and in the types of physical intimacy that they enjoy. And you've also seen how those things vary across time in the same relationship.

In this chapter we'll pick up on this theme again as we consider the answers to one of the main questions that we asked people: 'Who is the most important person in your life?' You'll see that answers vary widely. Some people prioritise their partner, but many see other people in their life as equally – or more – important.

This brings us to another key finding of the research – that there's some kind of 'third element' in most people's relationships that helps to sustain them over time. These third elements work in a similar way to the third leg on a stool; they help to stabilise it. You can imagine what would happen to a two-legged stool!

Here we'll explore several different third elements which people say are important in their relationships. For parents, the third element is often their children. For some people pets are crucial. For others, religion is the vital third element. For some

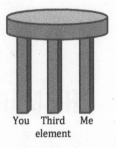

You   Third   Me
element

it's their interests or hobbies. For many people the crucial third element is their friends. For some people in non-monogamous relationships, it's their other partners. We'll look at all of these in more detail, and help you to think about the third elements in your own relationship – or what you might like them to be.

The third leg of the stool

Try this quiz yourself.

Here's a summary of what people in our research said, in answer to this question.

> ### VITAL STATISTICS:
>
> #### Who is your most important person?
>
> Everyone in our research had a current partner because that was what we were focusing on. However, only around two-thirds of them said that their partner was the most important person in their lives. Parents were less likely than others to name their partner as their most important person. They were just as likely to name their children.
>
> As we mentioned in Chapter 1, around one in ten of people who didn't have children said that the most important person in their life was themselves, and similar numbers of them said that it was another family member such as a parent or sibling. Just under 2 per cent of them listed a friend as the most important person in their lives.

QUIZ TIME: MOST IMPORTANT PEOPLE

1. Who is the most important person in your life? (tick only one)

My child/ren   A friend   My partner   A parent   A sibling
Myself   Another family member(s)   Other (say who) _____

2. Can you explain why?

_____

_____

_____

_____

We found that people who saw their partner or themselves as their most important person tended be more satisfied with their relationships and with their life in general than those who selected children.

There were also some interesting gender differences between parents in terms of who they saw as their most important person. More mothers named their children than their partners, but for fathers this was the opposite way around, with more of them naming their partners than their children.

Also, as children got older, parents were less likely to identify them as most important. Over three-quarters of mothers and over half of fathers said that children younger than nine years old were the most important people in their lives, but that went down significantly by the time children were eighteen years old – particularly so for fathers. As children became young adults, parents tended to name partners as the most important person again.

Many people reported that they'd found it really hard to choose who their most important person was, because it forced them to prioritise one person over all others. You might well have found it difficult yourself. Feelings can't always be so easily divided, measured and compared in this way. Most of us just don't have this kind of a hierarchy of emotions but rather we have several people in our lives who are equally important.

People also often spoke of having intertwined relationships rather than just one that they could pull out as the *most* important. Networks like these might include extended family, a friendship group, or a community based around a shared religion or set of interests, for example.

Think for yourself about whether it's relatively easy for you to put the people in your life in some kind of hierarchy. If so, on what basis do you do this? Is it about how close you feel to the person, how much time you spend with them, or some other measure? If you struggled with this is it because you relate more with the idea of intertwined relationships or networks? Or is it that you have a number of separate relationships in your life that give you different things? We'll come back to this towards the end of the chapter.

My number one?

People who did pick their partner as their most important person often did so because their lives together were particularly embedded – because, perhaps, they felt dependent on them, or their partnership or marriage was very much the main relationship in their life. This relationship gave them a sense of meaning and purpose. They often spoke about having gone through 'thick and thin' together with their partner or having worked through the kinds of 'ups and downs' that were perhaps less common in their friendships or family relationships. They used phrases such as 'other half' or 'an extension of me' to describe their partner. We'll come back to these ideas in the next chapter:

'Because she is literally my other half. I have lived with her over half my life.'

'After five years together, with so much love and affection shared and so many in-jokes, routines, experiences etc. it just feels like we have created our own private universe. It's hard to think of anything (or anyone) beyond that universe, which is the great constant in my life.'

There's quite a lot of debate over the role of partner relationships in people's lives these days. Some authors argue that romantic and sexual relationships have become more and more important to people, almost like a 'new religion' which people look to in order to fulfil all of their needs. Such writers say that people expect their partners to be 'everything' to them: their best friend, their lover, their co-parent, their confident, their cheer-leader, and so on.

However, other authors argue that people have recently become a lot more independent, autonomous, and focused on themselves as individuals – possibly more so than ever before. They claim that people now treat relationships as if they're disposable, focusing on their personal goals in life rather than on finding mutual aims and sharing a life together with a partner. Such authors highlight high divorce rate as evidence that people have less commitment to their relationships. They also argue that the increasing numbers of people who live alone (around a third of adults in the UK) suggests that not everyone is in – or even wants to be in – a relationship.

Some writers also suggest that relationships with children have now replaced those with partners as the most unconditional and reliable source of love and meaning in people's lives. They say some people are beginning to expect children to provide all of their needs in the way that people used to do with partners.

Which of these three things rings true in your life: Are partner relationships vitally important to you? Perhaps your own goals and the freedom to pursue them are equally, or more, important? Does the relationship that you have – or might have in future – with children provide your most heart-felt relationship anchor?

Our findings suggest that, for most people, *all* of these things are actually true. Many people are still deeply invested in their partner relationships, *and* they also feel the pressure to focus on individual goals, *and* they invest heavily in their relationships with children if they have them. We saw some of the conflicts that parents experienced over balancing these competing demands back in Chapter 3.

The impact of all of these competing pressures is that people have increasingly varied priorities, and diverse ways of doing relationships. As we've seen, many people do still prioritise their partner over all others, but nearly as many parents prioritise their children, and there are those who prioritise themselves or other friends and family too.

The third element

Even those who selected partners as their most important person also generally had at least one 'third element' in their relationship that helped to stabilise it. However, the ways in which the 'third element' works is different for different people.

For some people the stabilising aspect of the third element is having something which you share as a couple – like children, pets, religion, or a shared interest or activity. Many people place a lot of emphasis on sharing values, beliefs, tastes, ambitions and pastimes with their partner, seeing these as a key thing that connects them together.

For others it's more important that they each have some separate third element in their lives as individuals. This can help them to maintain independence and autonomy. It can also relieve the pressure on a partner to meet all of their needs. For example, if you can go train-spotting with a friend, watch horror movies with your sister, have gossipy conversations with your work colleague, go on a cycling holiday with your ex, do an art class on your own, and be silly and cuddly with your children, it matters less if your partner doesn't share your enjoyment of one or all of these things.

For many people it's about having both: some third elements which connect them together *and* some which they independently enjoy. Think back to your answers to the 'try it yourself' activity in Chapter 1, and the quiz in Chapter 2, about how important togetherness and separateness are for you. This will help you to consider how the ideas here apply in your own life: the kinds of together and separate third elements that you might value. Are there some things that immediately jump out at you as being crucial third elements in your relationships?

Now we'll cover some of the most common kinds of third elements that people see as important: children and companion animals; beliefs and interests; friends and other partners.

Parenting and pets

As you've seen, many parents – particularly mothers – see their children as being more important to them than their partners. People who have children clearly value them as significant relationships in their own right, but many also acknowledge the ways in which children bond them together as partners. Companion animals can also be important members of a family, and relationships in their own right as well.

Baby makes three?

In previous chapters you've seen how parenting shapes people's experiences and perceptions of their relationships. If you remember, we found that people without children are generally happier with their relationships than parents are. Parents do less 'relationship work' than people without children – probably due to all of the competing demands on their time. Parents in male–female relationships are the least likely to be there for each other and to make the kind of 'us-time' we spoke about in Chapter 1. They're also less likely to pursue shared interests, to say 'I love you', and to talk openly to one another (see Chapter 2). In Chapter 4 we also saw how many parents struggled to find opportunities for sex and other kinds of physical intimacy. Parents say things like: *'It is hard to make time to be with each other with children and work commitments.'*

It's not surprising that so many relationship self-help books emphasise the need to nurture the partner relationship as well as nurturing children! Interestingly, despite being less positive about their relationships than other people, mothers say that they're happier with their lives in general than anybody else. Putting this together with the 'most important person' findings, it does seem that children are a key source of happiness in the lives of many mothers rather than their partners.

As with so much that we've covered in this book, different people gave different reasons for why their children were so important to them. If you have children yourself, think about what they mean to you before reading on. Was having a child a deliberate decision for you or not? What does having a child bring to your life? What are the main challenges? If you have a co-parent – or more than one – would they say the same things as you or different things?

Some people emphasise the importance of blood ties and their child being a part of themselves. However, whether biologically linked or not, parents generally see the parent–child bond as a fundamental and elemental one. Many say that their love for a child, and the love they receive back, is *unconditional* and therefore different to other kinds of love. Some emphasise that the parent–child relationship is lifelong and therefore more secure than a partner relationship, which feels more likely to break-down, or end due to the death of one partner. For example, one person said:

'I could never walk away. I can imagine my relationship not working in the very long term, but I can't imagine not being part of my children's lives.'

Many people feel that children give their own lives meaning and purpose, for example: *'Because my son is the reason for being.'*

The decision to have a child, and the arrival of this new dimension in the relationship, were key points in the stories that people told us about their relationships. Having a child was a positive commitment – on a deeper level – to a mutual 'life project', showing their dedication to their relationship and their optimism that it would continue. Parenting was a joint venture and it gave partners the possibility of life enduring even beyond their relationship.

Of course parenting can, and often does, put immense pressure on relationships too. It can threaten the bond between partners just as much as it can stabilise it. It's important to remember that people have massively different experiences of parenting. As with the cultural expectations on romantic relationships, which we'll come to in Chapter 6, the idealised messages that we get about the 'wonders of parenthood' can put huge demands on us if we have children.

Many people don't get an instant bond with their child, and many don't find that parenthood brings the much-promised sense of meaning and purpose in life. Lack of sleep and the stresses of caring for a completely dependent being can feel completely overwhelming at times. This period of life can also feel very isolating because people still don't speak openly about the difficulties that so many of us face on the journey to becoming parents – such as infertility and miscarriage. It often feels like a path that partners have to walk alone, with all the pain and loss that's involved.

If you have children yourself think for a moment about the impact it's had on your relationship – in positive and negative ways. Did it bring you closer together with a partner, or push you further apart, or both? What about the impact on the other relationships in your life?

Sue and Ken's discussion of parenting includes both positive and negative aspects. It's clear that they see their children as bonding them together in the joint project of 'bettering themselves' – by enhancing their personal circumstances. At the same time they're aware that having children has closed off some opportunities, setting them on a different track to the one they might have otherwise chosen.

> **Ken:** Things might have been different in the sense that we obviously wanted to better ourselves for the children. Otherwise we might not have moved over here.
>
> **Sue:** We would have had no need for a three-bedroom house.
>
> **Ken:** Where would we have been? We moved here because we wanted the boys to go to a better school than the other place. We didn't need to move, the reason for moving was for the boys.
>
> **Sue:** It was entirely, yes.
>
> **Ken:** The house we had was fine for us. We probably wouldn't have had a mortgage now because we probably would have had enough money to pay it off.

Like Ken and Sue, quite a number of people in our research reflected on the ways in which children impacted on their living situation. This links back to some of the conversations we included in Chapter 2. For example, one single mother talked about the changes in her relationship when her partner moved in with her.

> *'I used to go round to his place and it was respite, being a single mum with kids. I'd go round on a Friday and he'd run a bath for me and there'd be candles around it and it used to be really lovely. You don't do that now!'*

Clearly, the experience of having children has the potential both for bringing parents closer together and for pushing them further apart. For example, there are often tensions in relationships when one person sees a child as the most important person in their life and the other sees this role still fulfilled by a partner. If one of you foregrounds their role as a parent and the other their role as a partner, this can become a point of distance or conflict between you. Differences of this kind can be particularly marked for second-time rounders and in step-parent families. However managing such differences and tensions can actually help to strengthen a relationship – as this mum indicates when describing what her partner does that makes her feel appreciated.

'He loves and treats my children (from my first marriage) just as he does his own.'

There may also be rifts if you have quite different ideas about how parenting should be done when it comes to issues such as discipline, schooling, or time spent together.

Some parents feel that children bring them closer together through the shared experience of watching them grow up and dealing with their crises. Children can also bring new possibilities into the family. Anish and Arundhati frequently spoke about the things that their children had picked up which helped all of them in their relationship. We mentioned how their daughter got them all exchanging little gifts in Chapter 1. Here they reflect on another example where she brought an element of celebration and appreciation into their daily lives.

Anish: Aiswari, our youngest daughter, is the one who picks up those ideas. She says, 'what are the three best things you did today?' So I tell her all the stupid things. Then she's a patient daughter: 'Oh, Daddy, you should say something serious.'
Arundhati: 'Say something real.'

Anish: These are the moments when the family gels together.

Arundhati: Yes you don't need Diwali or Christmas for that.

Animal magic

So we've seen that children can be a source of deep pleasure and joy that enhances people's relationships. However, parent–child relationships aren't the only kinds of relationships that can enrich our partnerships. Although we didn't list animals as one of the possible 'significant others' in our question about the most important person, many people spoke about their pets in similar ways to the ways in which others spoke about their children.

Over half of all British households include at least one pet, so sharing your life with an animal is an experience that many of us share. Dogs and cats are the most popular, in terms of the number of households which have them, but many people have fish (in tanks or ponds), rabbits, chickens, caged birds, guinea pigs, hamsters and other rodents, and reptiles. Also popular, but not quite as common, are horses and insects.

We often think about pets just in terms of the human needs which they fulfil: having something to cuddle and cheer you up, for example. But recently, writers have begun to see companion animals as significant others in their own right, members of the extended family alongside human kin. We were struck by just how many of the diaries that people kept included images of their pets.

Think about whether any animals would have a place in your own list of important significant others, if you were to broaden this out beyond human beings.

These two images, and their captions, show what an integral part of the home some cats were (see Chapter 2).

'Moggy putting herself on the emotion map!'

'Cat and detritus from our tea.'

Animals are often a source of the kind of everyday relationship communication that we discussed in Chapter 3, as the following picture shows. Both partners included this picture to illustrate the joke they enjoy sharing; how their pet is a ferocious guard dog – not! Lots of people shared news and images of pets with their partners and others over social media as well.

'The ferocious guard dog.'

Again, there are many different ways in which people share their lives with animals, and relationships with pets have different meanings for different people. For example, you might have specific roles about who looks after which pet or which pet is really 'yours'. A dog can bring two families together if they share caring for them, or walk them together. Many people have whole communities based around their animals. For example, in the 'crazy cat lady' social-networking group, people around the world share cat photos and videos and get advice from each other if a pet is ill or acting strangely. Do you connect with other people through animals in any of these kinds of ways?

We found that pets were particularly important for people without children and those whose children had left home. In these situations animals were sometimes a substitute or stand-in for children. Ella and Russell certainly expressed their relationship with their dog in similar ways to the way many parents described their children.

> **Ella:** The dog's just part of the family really. She's not quite 'our baby'! But if any of the animals were going to be, she would be it.
>
> **Russell:** There's unconditional love coming back from her.

Mona reflects on her and Chloe's ideas about getting a dog or a child, in the same thought process:

> *'I think it would be a good thing whether we had children or whether we had a dog. Obviously there's going to be issues, there always is, because I watch my brother and my mates who have kids and you're so tired because you've got to stay up with the puppy or the baby and you're bereft of sleep. You just find the inner strength and you have to rely on each other a lot more, with a lot less patience with everything. There would be challenges but it would be a positive, definitely a positive.'*

For partners who're thinking about having children, the decision to get a pet together can be a helpful first step in committing to a shared life project that includes having a dependent. Conversations about raising an animal can be a way of testing the water on their commitment levels, or they can be a way of putting off a conversation about when to start a family.

However, many people valued animals as important in their own right. Several people spoke about how their pets gave them an alternative listening ear: somebody who could be there when their partner couldn't, or someone they could run things past before talking to their partner. Pets could also be mediators in a relationship, helping partners to manage or avoid conflict. For example a person might direct a comment to their pet – within earshot of a partner – 'somebody's grumpy today' or 'shall we go out and get some fresh air?' Some people found that pets picked up on their emotional state, signalling when they were heading for an argument. A pet's distress, in these circumstances, could make them take some time out instead of continuing to fight. Walking the dog or feeding the rabbit can also be a good excuse for taking a break from an argument.

In many ways animals create a sense of home and family. Esther and Alan put it very clearly:

Esther: Oh, we can't have a house without a pet in it. It's empty.

Alan: It's part of the family, an animal. To me it is. Always has been.

Esther: You can tell them things you wouldn't tell somebody else.

Alan: Yes, you can talk to them.

Esther: They'll sit at your feet but you can talk to them. They don't tell secrets and things like that.

Alan: That's right, they don't.

Like children, pets can bring the past, present and future of our lives together. Animals can link us back to our childhoods as we try to recreate past experiences in our current relationship, or, maybe we get a pet because that wasn't possible when we were kids. The times when pets joined a relationship, and the scrapes and incidents in the lives of our animals, often become important shared memories which we tell together, for example, the way that our dog 'chose us' at the rescue centre or the funny things the cat used to do when it was a kitten. Pets can also be a way of showing that we're committed to a joint future together in our relationship.

Everyday rituals of caring for animals can also become a kind of relationship work that bonds us together with a partner, as Janet illustrates here when she speaks about how their dog opened up the opportunity for both time together and time apart in her relationship.

Walking the dog. We do that together and alone, which is nice.

However, it's important to remember that, like children, pets can also create stress as well as pleasure. It can be tough if people have different feelings around animals, for example if only one person wants a pet, if you can't afford an animal, or if one person is a 'dog person' and the other a 'cat person'. Hugh alluded to this when he said: *'We don't have any pets. I think Rose would love a dog.'*

As with the other sources of conflict that we spoke about in Chapter 3, how we deal with these kinds of differences can help to consolidate our relationships or they can open up wider areas of tension and disagreement. As with parenting, if an animal is seen as taking the kind of love, affection or time that one of us would really like to get from our partner this can become a bone of contention. Conflict can also bubble up around who does the bulk of the work with the animals. There's also the painful fact that bereavement is inevitable with animals because they have significantly shorter lifespans than humans – giant tortoises being pretty uncommon pets! However, situations like these can also give us the possibility to come together and support each other too.

So while pets may seem trivial and perhaps unlikely third dimensions in couple relationships, they can be incredibly important for some people. Before moving on, think some more about the role of animals in your own relationship. Do any of the stories here sound familiar to you? If you don't have any pets, would you like to get one, now or in future? What would this mean for you?

> **TOP TIP**
>
> If you have animals, think about the ways that you spend time with them within your relationships. Often this is probably rather mundane and everyday, but could you create some special time for this once in a while? It might be taking the dog for a walk or snuggling up with the cat, watching the fish together, or teaching the parrot a new word!
>
> If you don't have animals (or even if you do) perhaps you could bring animals into your life in another way: visit a local farm or wildlife centre, feed the birds, or go on a walk where you note down all the wild animals you see (you can even create a scoring system based on how rare or cute they are!). Or you could borrow a pet from a friend for a day to see what it's like.

Beliefs and interests

You might remember that 'shared values and interests' is one of the very top things that people like about their relationships (see Chapter 3). Lots of people say that it's important to share their faith, beliefs, tastes, ambitions and interests with their partner.

Similarly, people seem to really dislike it when they don't have many shared values and interests. They often feel uneasy if there are major differences between them, especially about faith or political views. Several people said that having opposing beliefs and values adversely affected their relationship.

Before we look at religion and leisure pursuits in a bit more detail, think about what the important beliefs and interests are in your own life. Consider religion and spirituality, politics and activism, opinions and attitudes, interests and hobbies, and tastes and preferences. Which of these are most important to you? Is it important that these things are something you share – or keep separate – from your partner?

Religion and community

Around 40 per cent of the people in our research had some kind of religious belief. This group of people were, on average, slightly happier with their lives than people who weren't religious, and most other research in this area finds this as well. This is probably to do with the sense of meaning that religion can give people, as well as the supportive communities that a lot of people get through their faith. Religious people were also slightly more likely to spend time on their relationships, although they weren't any more satisfied with their relationships than anybody else.

You won't be surprised to hear, by this stage, that 'being religious' means different things to different people, and that religion features differently in different relationships. Some people say that their faith gives them a useful template for how to live their relationships. The doctrines and scriptures of many religions provide guidance about relationships, such as what partners should promise to each other, and what the purpose of a relationship should be. For example, Thomas said that the sacrament of the Christian marriage ceremony – 'till death do us part' – was an ever-present reminder for him that he had to work hard at his relationship. This was something that he could hang on to through difficult times.

It can feel difficult to navigate relationships without this sense of having a map or a rulebook to guide you. This might explain the popularity of self-help books on relationships among people who don't have a faith or spiritual belief. It can be reassuring to be told the 'right' way to do relationships, and to feel that this is sanctified by a higher power of some kind. For some people, therefore, it's clear that God is the third party in their relationship: the stabilising third leg of their stool. As Thomas and Christy say:

Christy: We believe that this God is the God that created everything. As you grow closer to God, you grow closer to each other as well, because God's ways are your ways then.

Thomas: There's three of us with God, but it's not crowded at all!

In addition to God, religions give many people another third element to their relationship in the form of a community network through their local mosque, synagogue, chapel, Buddhist centre, or similar. For example, Linda and James's relationship was embedded within their family, which was, in turn, embedded within the church community. Linda said: '*We go to church, see other people from church.*'

Religion can also help people to structure their lives together. As Anish mentioned earlier, religion provides his family with specific points in the year for celebration together. Religions also create opportunities for commemorating the partnership (marriage, anniversaries, etc.) and daily practices in the form of prayer, meditation, shared meals, and so on. Margaret linked the faith that she and Martin share with how easy it feels for them to navigate their everyday life, such as shopping.

'*Quakers live very simply and they don't put a lot of store by consumer goods and so on: the latest and the best. So we just bought second-hand stuff. I think we're fairly in agreement over things like that.*'

However, this isn't to say that religion is a bonding element in all relationships. When partners have different beliefs or different interpretations of the same beliefs, it can be a major source of tension. For other people, it can be valuable that they have *different* beliefs because their separate religions give them each some time apart and provide a sense of belonging to something other than the relationship.

So for many people religion is important to their relationships, but it works in different ways for different people. Do you have a faith, religion, or spiritual practice? Or is it perhaps important to you that you're agnostic or atheist? Do you prefer a partner to share your beliefs – or does this not matter? Does having a religion, or not, impact on your relationships?

Hobbies and activities

Of course having a sense of community isn't unique to people with religious beliefs. For example, same-sex partners might find that local LGBT centres and bars, events such as Pride marches, and online LGBT networks work in a similar way for them, giving them a sense of a wider like-minded community. Other people find community through politics, interests or hobbies. These kinds of communities often give partners a structure to their days, years, and lives together, for example, through regular gaming nights, annual conventions, or something important that they build towards – like competing in a marathon or standing for election.

We already saw, in Chapter 1, how people value pastimes and interests both as something they can do together and as something they can do separately: a form of 'us-time' and 'me-time'. For example, Linda and James spoke about how there were forms of physical activity which they shared with each other and with their daughter, and some that they did separately.

Linda: I used to exercise and I want to go back to it. It's finding the time now. This has been the longest I've not had a gym membership or gone to an exercise class. It's always been something important to me. When I was pregnant I even went to yoga and all of that and I felt quite fit. Everything's slowed down now. I really would like to go back and do something. I miss it.

James: I've got swimming with her.

Linda: You've got that bike.

James: We're going to be biking all over the place because she's got a bike now.

Similarly, Eleri and Alun spoke about food and wine as an important shared interest which they enjoy together. Its relationship value was such that they felt it was worth spending money on, as were their separate interests in music and books. Being careful with money is important for them and they both cherish having something in their lives that involves some expense – but not too much.

Eleri: I think we're quite similar in what we think is expensive and what we think is important to buy. We'll go out for a meal for a birthday but we don't spend a lot of money on clothes. We don't buy lots of material things, really. Some of our friends will go out shopping every week for clothes. We don't do that kind of thing.

Alun: My computer and all the stuff I use for recording is probably the most expensive thing. But I've accumulated that over years and I've done it—

Eleri: —sensibly.

Alun: We're careful, really.

Eleri: I buy lots of books.

Alun: But that's your job, you need stuff.

One of the ways we explored people's everyday lives in our research was using relationship diaries. These help people to see how their relationships are shaped by the kinds of third elements that we're talking about here. Here's how to do it.

TRY IT YOURSELF: RELATIONSHIP DIARY

Diaries aim to find out about your everyday routines, that is, what you do and when day by day. You can use a diary to reflect on any aspect of your relationship during the week, writing as little or as much as you like.

The diary can also become a kind of scrapbook. You can include mementos of the time you spend together. This might be TV guide clippings or receipts for the cinema, for example, or maybe the label from a bottle of wine or beer, a menu from a meal out or takeaway, or the packaging from a shared meal at home.

The diary format is flexible. You can use a notebook, a document on a computer, a calendar on your phone, a blog or social-media site, or a cardboard box which you put things in. Use whatever works for you. You can also take photos on your phone and attach these or print them out.

You can include your experiences of some or all of the following areas:

- Any time that you spend together, including the kinds of activities you do, the times of day and how long it lasts
- Any time that you spend apart, including the kinds of activities you do, the times of day and how long it lasts
- Any things, both inside and outside the home that make you think about, or affect, your relationship in some way (such as your job, TV programmes, etc.)
- Any conversations or contact with people who make you think about, or affect, your relationship in some way (such as your family, friends, children, etc.)
- Anything that you or your partner do for each other (such as gestures, actions, words)
- Anything that you do for yourself
- One good moment from each day
- One challenging moment from each day

As with the emotion maps in Chapter 2, once you've kept your diary for a week you can look through it and then write a final entry about some of the things that stand out for you. Is there something that you or your partner does which is especially important for you? Or maybe there's something that's particularly annoying? What kinds of things come up frequently – like the cups of tea in our research?

You and a partner can keep separate diaries and then compare them or you could try making one together and chatting at the end of each day about what you want to include. It's up to you how you do it; the idea is just to help you to explore the day-to-day activities and interactions that shape your lives.

Friends and partners

Although only a small proportion of people in our research said that friends were *more* important than their partners, it's clear that many people have friends who are integral to their lives. Indeed, networks of friendships are often something that sustain people's partner relationships.

Some people spoke about how they couldn't prioritise partners over friends, or vice versa, because both were equally important. For example, they might have had friends who they'd known for a lifetime, or who had seen them through difficult times or previous relationships. Some people share confidences with friends which they can't share with their partners or which their partners aren't really interested in. People in openly non-monogamous relationships often have multiple close people in their lives at the level of partner, or find that boundaries between friends and partners are blurred. We'll say a bit more about all of these things in a moment.

The value of friendship

Before we start, think about the role of friendship in your own life. Are friendships important to you? If so, which kinds of friends (e.g., old friends, friends who are also colleagues, friends you see regularly)? What role do you think that friendships have in your partner relationships?

As always it's clear from our research that friendships have different roles in different relationships. Some key examples are:

- Friendships can relieve pressure on a partner to meet all of each other's needs
- Friends provide support in times of relationship conflict or crisis
- Friends often help partners to celebrate the good times in their relationship
- Joint friendships can enable partners to share activities with other individuals or couples
- Groups of friends can provide a network of shared values and interests around the relationship

Janet and Robert, for example, spoke about the fact that friendships often came into their lives through Janet who was the most outgoing of the pair. These female friendships met some of Janet's needs that weren't being met by Robert due to his 'homebody' character, while Robert found that he enjoyed being encouraged to socialise in this way.

> **Janet:** I think Robert is a real homebody: he loves being at home; he loves the home comforts. I could be out every night: I would love it. And when I was at work Robert didn't really mind. There were quite a lot of glasses of wine after work. I always made a nice girlfriend wherever I worked and they became our friends. And they still are our friends.
>
> **Robert:** But I always join in quite regularly.

Another good example of friends meeting needs which a partner can't came from Leona, who we met at the end of Chapter 3. You might remember that when her father died Leona's partner found it hard to empathise with her. Turning to a friend who had been through the same thing was a huge support and diffused an otherwise emotionally difficult situation. She sums it up nicely:

You can't be the perfect person and supply the other person with everything they need, it's absolutely impossible.

We'll come back, in the next chapter, to the common assumption that a partner should meet all of our needs, and the impact that this has on relationships. For now, reflect on your own needs and the ways that these are met by friends, family and other important people in your life, in addition to partners.

Christine emphasised the value of friends and family in getting her and Moira through the tough times in their relationships. She wasn't even sure whether they would have stayed together without this support: *'If it was just on our own, who knows? Would we have done it?'*

For Christine both the emotional and practical support that friends gave her at difficult times was invaluable to her relationship. Emotionally, our friends can give us a listening ear or advice about what's worked for them in similar circumstances. Practically, they can give us a room for the night if one of us needs some space, or financial support or childcare to ease some of the pressure when we're struggling.

Some people tend to withdraw and pull up the emotional drawbridge in times of crisis, because they're embarrassed to admit that they're struggling. However, the experience of people like Moira and Christine suggests that it's worth trying to remain more open when you're having a hard time, and to let friends in. All relationships go through difficult times and that support can make all the difference.

Several partners also spoke of the value of having people who were friends with both of them. James and Linda, and Manuel and Oscar, had friends who they were close to who were perhaps more like family members.

> **James:** Camilla, well she's actually both of our friend but more Linda's childhood friend. She was involved with us on these committees that we used to be on when we lived in the old neighbourhood.

> **Oscar:** I think Sofia's probably our closest friend. Both our closest friend, would you agree?
> **Manuel:** Yes
> **Oscar:** We had met each other but not really noticed each other. Then she organised some kind of reunion and sent me a message on the social network. And we quite liked each other, and exchanged very long messages, and grew very close very quickly. And then she also met Manuel and grew close to him as well. Then she basically lived with us for half a year or so. And the funny thing was that she never had any clothing in our place. She always just wore my T-shirts! We're considering moving in with her and Ben. It has a very special feel when we're with her. It's a very old dynamic, and something I enjoy very much. I think it's something we all get a lot of energy from.
> **Manuel:** Yes.
> **Oscar:** When we're down and then we meet, we feel much, much better. We can laugh together, we can talk about anything, we can just open up. And also we already share so much history and knowledge which we can build. I think it's really something extremely rare. Just being together is something that really helps us all.

It's clear from these examples that close friendships can really nourish a partnership, perhaps bringing out sides of each person that don't surface when it's just the two of them.

Manuel and Oscar became more of a three-legged stool with Sofia, and there's a possibility of them developing even stronger connections in the future if they decide to combine their lives and move in together.

Finally, many people spoke more about networks of friendship than they did about specific friends. For example, Emma and Jake have regular contact with a wider group which enables them to enjoy their shared interests with like-minded people.

> **Emma:** We have a group of friends that we alternate with. Every month we'll go over to one person's house to watch classic Doctor Who episodes, because they're a bunch of geeks.
>
> **Jake:** You're there along with them, sweetie!

Of course, friendships aren't without their difficulties. In all of the situations here, tensions could crop up. For example, if one person felt that they should meet all of their partner's needs, they could come to resent their partner's friendships. In Leona's case she said that it was crucial that her partner wasn't jealous, given that she was getting a lot of support and emotional closeness from another man. For some people, letting friends in when they're struggling just feels too vulnerable. There's also a risk that friends will take sides and make matters worse rather than better.

As in all relationships, it can be tough when friendships change or end over time. For example, Oscar and Manuel might find it tough if they didn't get on with Ben; Jake and Emma might struggle if people in their friendship group started having children and had less time for their monthly get-togethers, or if some of them fell out with each other.

Unlike romantic relationships there's often far less of a script for how to deal with friendships changing and ending, and this can make things tricky. Partners may find it difficult that their relationship is forced to change if a once-close friend moves away or if their community disappears, for example, and suddenly some of their needs are no longer being met through friends. Think about how the friendships in your life have changed over time, and how you've managed this. Have changes in friendships had an impact on your partner relationships?

> **TOP TIP**
>
> Over the next month make one time to spend with friends that connects to your partner relationship, and one that's separate from it.
>
> For example, if you have a partner, the connected time might be having another couple round for dinner, or doing something you both enjoy with a friend who shares your interests. If you don't have a partner, connected time might be chatting to a friend about how you're both feeling about relationships at the moment, going to watch a romantic comedy and chatting about it after, or going speed-dating together.
>
> The separate time could be anything that you and your friend enjoy doing together that isn't connected to romantic relationships, or that your partner – if you have one – doesn't get. If you don't have that kind of friendship at the moment then perhaps sign up for a one-off class or group outing with other people who enjoy that thing.

Other significant others

So far in this book we haven't said much about people who're in openly non-monogamous relationships. We did touch briefly on *secret* non-monogamy – often known as infidelity. For example, you might remember how Peter's partner, in Chapter 3, struggled with his watching Internet porn, seeing it as a form of cheating. And Leona, in the previous section, was relieved that her partner didn't see her close friendship with another guy as a kind of infidelity. Another person in our research, Paul, said that the value of friendship for him was that his friends pulled him up when he was having an affair, out of their loyalty to his partner. It was them telling him to 'get his act together' that helped him to end the affair and to repair the damage it caused. This same group of friends then rallied around the couple to support them through their tough time.

However, in addition to secret non-monogamy, there are also many forms of *open* non-monogamy such as polyamory or open relationships where people are honest about the fact that they have more than one sexual partner or emotionally close person in their lives.

Overall, around 5 per cent of relationships are openly non-monogamous in some way (and up to two-thirds are secretly non-monogamous at some time). In our study a number of people spoke about having more than one partner, or about having sexual contact with people in addition to their partner. You might remember, for example, Anna from Chapter 2, who wanted to have a big-enough house so that she and her partner could invite their mutual friend and sexual partner around to stay, or the couple from Chapter 4 who occasionally had sex together with an escort. These are examples of open relationships, or swinging, where a couple has sex – together or separately – with other people.

Not all open non-monogamy is focused on sex. For polyamorous people, like Joss and Jake, the focus is on having more than one close relationship, which may or may not be sexual. For example Joss explained how her other partners were not quite the same as friends:

'When I was seeing Claire quite regularly I think our son picked up that she was in a different category from Mummy's other friends. I think he had her in a different category in his head.'

Some polyamorous people, like Joss and Jake, have one primary partner and other relationships which are more secondary. This is sometimes called *hierarchical* polyamory. Others have more than one equal partner (*egalitarian* polyamory) where they might live together in a triad or a quad, for example. Alternatively, one person might value their independence – perhaps living alone but have several partners who they visit and who visit them – this is known as *solo poly*. *Relationship anarchists* question why we have hierarchies between friends and partners at all. They just have many close people in their lives and don't really draw distinctions between them, for example, in terms of whether they have sex together or not.

Like Jake and Joss, Emmie and Theo have the more hierarchical version of polyamory. They see themselves as a couple, and each other as their main source of comfort, but importantly both of them can see other people and they have a mutual lover in David. Emmie said:

> *'The important bit is that the rules stay the same for both of us: we can both have other partners but we have to be open and honest about it. You see that in the relationship with David, that's exactly what we do. It's that kind of openness, that kind of honesty that is really at the heart of our relationship. If we talk through things, if we don't hide anything from each other that gives us a solid foundation, that kind of trust. It's a comfort zone in a sense. I know that I can go to Theo and there will always be something comfortable there. Whatever madness is going on around me, there's always comfort in his arms.'*

This kind of openness doesn't mean that 'anything goes': on the contrary open non-monogamy, like monogamy, takes plenty of relationship work. Emmie and Theo stressed the role of trust and honest communication in sustaining their relationship, but they also spoke about much more everyday practices. Going back to our perennial example of the cup of tea, one way in which Theo and Emmie mark the specialness of their relationship is by having their own mugs for tea which only they use, particularly after they've just had sex. Many other polyamorous people talk about of having certain practices or rituals that they use to signify the importance of their different relationships.

Marico has an egalitarian triadic model in his relationship with Daniel and Andreas, depicted here in his emotion map.

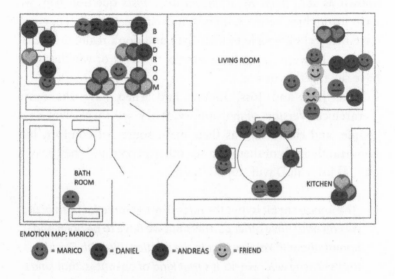

EMOTION MAP: MARICO

😊 = MARICO ⚫ = DANIEL ⚫ = ANDREAS 😊 = FRIEND

In his diary he describes some of their everyday life:

'Daniel fell asleep on the couch snuggled around Andreas. I then carried Daniel to bed, and we both kissed goodnight. That was a wonderful episode.

'Later that night I spent some time talking with Andreas about the events of the day to reflect on them and adapt communicative behaviour that might've led to unhappiness. We then discussed who was going to sleep where (the bed in the bedroom is too small for the three of us).

'After I had woken up the next morning, I had a shower. When I got out, Andreas had sent me a text that they were awake and I was free to join them in the bed. I did so, we cuddled a bit, and then we had breakfast.'

As with monogamous relationships, as you can see, people in openly non-monogamous relationships have many different ways of managing their relationships, their communication, and the ways they structure their households. There are many different kinds of open non-monogamy and even within each kind there's a diversity of ways of managing them. For example, some people want clear contracts of how to do things while others emphasise individual freedom, trusting each other to make good choices. Some tell each other everything whereas others value privacy within their various relationships.

Also, as with monogamous relationships, lovers and partners can take many different roles in sustaining and nurturing each other's relationships, including all of the ones that we've previously covered when we talked about friendship.

Of course, with non-monogamous relationships, there's also the potential for other partnerships to address the kinds of discrepancies in sexual desire that we covered in Chapter 4. People with different levels or types of sexual desire can more easily get these met if they have more than one lover.

Also, when people live with – or are close to – other partners, some of the burdens of domestic labour and childcare can be shared between greater numbers of people, just like with other kinds of extended family. Elizabeth Sheff's research on polyamorous families found that this was something they particularly benefited from, and we can see why given the stresses and struggles mentioned by many of the monogamous parents in our research.

Some authors are beginning to question the clear dividing lines that we often draw between monogamous and non-monogamous relationships, pointing to relationship styles like 'monogamish' relationships (which are somewhat open) or 'friends with benefits', which blur the lines between friends and partners. Perhaps relationships could be more usefully seen as a spectrum rather than an either/or thing. Whether you're monogamous or non-monogamous yourself, the following activity helps you think about the place of significant others in your life.

TRY IT YOURSELF: CONTINUUMS OF INTIMACY

Think about where you'd like to be on each of the continuums below. Draw an X at the point on the line where you think you'd generally like to be (of course this might alter over time).

Then think about where any past and current partners would be on these scales. Are you both in the same place? Or perhaps you're in different places? Is everyone content with where they are?

If it helps to think about specific examples the emotional closeness continuum could include: at the far left, just having one partner you talk with about everything and nobody else who feels that close. Towards the middle it could involve having several friends who are as close to you as your partner – those who you could call up at 3 a.m. or who you share something with every day. Towards the far right it might include very close relationships that you've retained with ex-partners, staying up all night talking with a person you've recently met, or living communally with several people.

The physical intimacy continuum could include things, on the far left, like only hugging your partner and no one else. Towards the middle might be things like being okay with fantasising about other people but not doing anything in reality, or perhaps having online sex. Towards the far right would be the kinds of open and polyamorous relationships that we've discussed in this section.

Continuum of emotional closeness

Monoamory	Polyamory

One close intimate relationship & no close relationships outside this	Multiple close relationships

Continuum of physical intimacy

Monosex	Polysex

No physical intimacy at all outside main relationship	Multiple sexual encounters

As in previous chapters the important thing to emphasise is that there's no 'right' or 'wrong' place to be on these continuums. Rather different things work for different people. If you find that you and a partner are in different places then it's good to talk things through rather than trying to figure out who is 'wrong' and trying to change them. Some of the advice about communication from Chapter 3 should be useful here, as should some of the resources mentioned at the end of Chapter 6.

Conclusions

From everything you've seen in this chapter, and before, there's clearly a huge diversity of ways to be a partner, to view relationships, and to manage relationships on a daily basis. Just consider the following:

- Whether you live together or not, and whether you live with other people or just with a partner.
- How much time you spend together and how you spend it, in person and online.

- Whether you see your partner as your most important person, or as equally important to, or less important than, others.
- Whether you have children and, if so, in what ways (adoption, fostering, or from giving birth yourself; having one child or multiple children; sharing parenting roles with one other adult or several; living as a single parent, two parent, or extended family).
- Whether you are monogamous, non-monogamous, or somewhere between the two.

Given this diversity it's clear that there's obviously no one-size-fits-all set of rules for doing relationships. There's no secret of enduring love, but rather many secrets. It's about finding out what works for you.

SUMMARY SUGGESTIONS: THE MAGIC NUMBER

Here are a few more things to try yourself, based on this chapter.

- Consider the idea of the third leg of a stool stabilising a relationship. Now you've read lots of examples, what would you say are the 'third elements' in your relationship? Have these changed over time? Which elements have remained constant and which have changed?
- Reflect on your relationship and parenthood. Do you have children? If so, which of the ideas in the section on parenting were familiar to you? If you don't have children is this something you'd like? Which of the various possible ways of including children in your relationship are you drawn to?
- Explore how important shared values are to you. People differ a lot in terms of how important it is that they share values and preferences with a partner. Consider which – if any – of the following are vital for you, and anything else that you think of: Religious beliefs – or not having religious

beliefs? Party politics or political allegiances? Shared views on child-rearing? Views on equality? Shared musical tastes? Preferred ways of socialising? Views on monogamy/non-monogamy?

- In this chapter we introduced you to the relationship diary. You could try keeping one for a week particularly focusing on any of the things we've covered here, or in other chapters.

- Place the different people (and non-human 'significant others') in your life within these circles. Put yourself in the centre and then add in others around you. You can include actual names or the kinds of relationship they have with you, as with the illustration here.

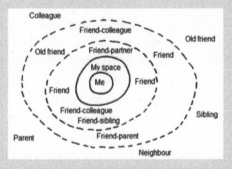

Now, using these concentric circles, think about how you determine who is closer or further away. Is it about the amount of time you spend together? Or perhaps it's the 'quality' of the time you spend together more than duration? Does whether you live together have an impact? Or maybe it's the kind of relationship it is (partner, family, friend, colleague etc.)? Perhaps it's about how long you've known someone, how close you feel to them, or how willing you are to let them see you when you're vulnerable? Or perhaps it's a combination of all of these things and more?

CHAPTER 6
YOUR LOVE STORY

There are all kinds of love in the world, but never the same love twice.

– F. Scott Fitzgerald

Over the course of this book we've explored many different aspects of our everyday relationships. We've covered the importance of small acts of kindness; how people occupy the spaces they live in; how they communicate with each other; the place of physical affection in their daily lives; and how their relationships are embedded within their families, wider networks and communities.

In this last chapter we're widening things out even further to consider how our everyday relationships fit into the bigger stories that we hear about love and romance. Movies, magazines, and advertisements generally show us a very narrow and idealised image of what relationships 'should' be like. Given the diversity of relationships that we've seen throughout this book, it's helpful to ask how we can tell our own relationships stories when these are bound to differ – often significantly – from the stories in the world around us. How do we describe our own relationships when they don't fit with the popular story of falling madly in love with our 'perfect match' and living together happily ever after?

We'll focus here particularly on what we mean when we talk about love. We'll also explore how you can tell your own 'love stories' in ways that include the difficult aspects of your relationships, the inevitable conflicts, tensions, and crises that happen along the way, and the times that threaten to tear you apart rather than bring you together. There isn't much of a script for how to manage such situations, and that can leave you feeling isolated and alone when the tough times hit. However, our research gave us many helpful ideas for how you can write your own love stories instead of trying to fit into the ones that are out there in the world.

As this is the last chapter of the book, we'll also bring everything together with a chance to reflect on what you've learnt over the course of the book and where you might go next if you'd like to continue the explorations you've started here.

Romance is dead: long live relationships?

The idealised messages that we receive about romantic love can put a lot of pressure on us, especially when it seems that our own relationship doesn't match up to them. There are certainly times when most of us fear that our relationship isn't good enough in one way or another. You might remember Daniela in Chapter 4, who was concerned that she and Darren weren't a 'proper couple' because they hadn't had much sex since their children came along. Or Jack's shocked response, in Chapter 2, when he found out that Ayesha would like to live separately. Given the strong expectation that people should move closer together over time, not further apart, Jack was worried about what his girlfriend's request meant for their relationship.

Message of love

So what are the common ideas that we get about love? Researchers have studied romantic comedies, relationship advice, and pop songs to explore the kinds of messages that surround us in our everyday lives. But you probably only need to think for a moment of the stories you heard growing up, the TV programmes you've recently watched, or the songs you hear on the radio, to come up with many of them yourself. Three main ones are: 'The One', the relationship escalator, and 'happily-ever-after'.

The common message – from fairy tales to situation comedies – seems to be that we need to find 'The One' true love who will 'complete us' and be our 'perfect match'. Single people are assumed to be unhappy, lonely and desperately searching for love. This perhaps explains why there are so many films about people finding a partner and far fewer devoted to people finding friendship, for example. Once we've found 'The One', we're supposed to want to stay 'together for ever', to be 'everything' to each other, to 'always' love each other, and to never want to be apart. Romantic love will 'conquer all' and 'save the day'.

The relationship escalator that we touched on in Chapter 1 is another common message. This is the assumption that once you get together with a partner it's like getting on an escalator where you're forced to keep going higher and higher in the same direction. There are no other possible directions. You can't go down an upwardly moving stairway. The relationship escalator takes people from dating to sex, to committing to each other and then moving in together, to marriage, to having children, and so on. There might be slight differences in the relationship escalators of different communities (based on religion or culture, for example), but they all move in the same direction – that is, increasingly sharing your life: pooling households, money and possessions, and making increasingly big commitments to bring you emotionally closer over time. The only way off the escalator is if one or both of you dies!

Finally, there's an assumption that people need to feel and behave in the same ways in their relationship over time. This is the ideal of 'happily ever after'. People should remain 'in love' and passionately sexual, they shouldn't need to go outside the relationship to get any of their needs met, and they shouldn't

have major conflicts. A change in any of these things is considered a 'bad sign', raising questions that can undermine the relationship: perhaps this person isn't 'The One' after all?

So a summary of the common messages might look something like this:

> *'You will both fall in love and be in love with each other for ever. You will live together and share all aspects of your lives. You shouldn't argue and you must telepathically know what each other wants. Your relationship should stay sexual – to keep the passion alive – and you should remain faithful to each other. You'll be the most important person for your partner – at least until children arrive – and together you'll meet all of each other's needs.'*

Hopefully laying these ideals out like this you can already see a few problems with them! The difficulty is that even though we might question them, they're often so omnipresent in the world around us that they create a powerful point of comparison. It's easy to find ourselves unwittingly holding our relationship up against the perfect image of the billboard advertisement couple, or the hot porn clip, or the lovers in the chicklit novel, for example.

There is no normal

It can be helpful to remind ourselves that such an idealised version of love is by no means a universal aspiration. It's not what everyone has always looked for over the course of history and it's not what everyone looks for around the world today. One size really doesn't come near to fitting all of us – why would it?

In her book, *Marriage, A History*, the historian Stephanie Coontz highlights the fact that it's only at this point in time that people in Western countries have aspired to the particular ideal of romantic love. Before the 1950s, marriage generally had much more to do with combining families together or matters of economy like work and child-rearing, for example. This isn't to say that people didn't fall in love or enjoy romance before the 1950s, but they were far less likely to look for one person to fulfil all of their needs for security, excitement, sex, belonging, partnership, self-validation, co-parenting, etc. etc. etc.

An idealised version of love came in because of changes in society such as the declining importance of religion, less stable jobs, and the fact that people started to move around during their lives rather than staying in small tightly knit families and communities. These shifts meant that people began to look to romantic relationships to meet needs that might have been previously met by other people or in other places. For example, when we don't get a sense of meaning, security and validation from a religion or career, we might turn to a partner to provide us with these things. Also, these days we tend to expect a partner to be a co-parent if we have children, and this can be a source of tension, as we saw in Chapter 3. At other points in time, childcare was shared out more between extended family and wider community.

As you read in Chapter 5, the expectation that romantic partners will meet all of our needs may also be changing again, with some people prioritising their own individual goals and dreams over their relationships, and others turning more towards their children as a source of meaning and unconditional love.

People in our research noticed how changes in relationships had happened over time – even within their own lifetimes. For example, Anne reflected on how the decisions that she and Henry made about their relationship had been solely down to them, without any involvement from their families. This was very different from their parents' experience:

'It's more individualised now. We've got more flexibility, like deciding to get married. I suppose I'm quite far away from my parents and they have no say.'

Another person described being a kind of intermediary between her parents' generation and her children's generation because the gulf between their understandings of relationships was so wide. It was down to her to bridge the generation gap. Her South Asian parents expected that they would have a big role in their children's choice of partners and they anticipated that they would all live together, as extended family, once these relationships were settled. In contrast, her children expected complete freedom to choose their own partners, and that they would live in a 'nuclear family' household. Her experience of how it feels to sit in the middle of such seismic generational shifts is a powerful one.

If we look around the world, as well as across time, we also see huge diversity in how people *do* their relationships.

Considering different cultures globally, or even within one country, there's a lot of variation. For example in:

- Whether love is seen as something you 'fall into', or whether a good match can be chosen – by friends, relatives, or Internet dating sites – with love blossoming over time.
- Whether people are expected to only have one partner at a time, or whether additional love relationships (in the form of affairs or mistresses, for example) or multiple partnerships (as in polygamous or polyamorous arrangements) are tolerated or even expected.

Several people picked up on these cultural differences and how they played out in their own relationships. For example, talking about the influence of Kenyan culture on their relationship, Georgina and Anton said:

Georgina: Anton helps a lot in the house. That's a way of saying 'I love you' I feel. He helps with the household chores: he hoovers and does the dishes.

Anton: Love is routinised in most African marriages. That means it's fulfilled in the relationship, and it's not verbalised. My view is love is expressed. You can say anything but you're not meaning it. I think this is what's happening in the Western world.

For Anton and Georgina, the idealised talk of love in Western cultures is just words. For them, the *feelings* come from the practices and routines of love. Similarly, some people in arranged marriages spoke of love as something that grows, getting stronger and richer over time. They see this as something quite different to Western 'love at first sight'.

Also, while the nuclear family of Mum, Dad and a couple of children is often presented as the norm in Western adverts, TV soap operas and the like, you'll remember that many people in our research have very different cultural experiences where extended families are the norm. We saw in Chapters 1 and 3 how such partners share space and time together but may rarely see themselves as a 'couple' or as needing 'us-time' in the way that other partners might expect.

Think for a moment about your own place in time and space. What ideas do you have about love and relationships because of the generational time and the geographical area that you live in? Does the time period you grew up in make a difference, or where your family came from originally, for example? How have the messages that you received about love in this time and space context influenced your own relationships?

These diverse cultural understandings and experiences demonstrate that love and partnership don't necessarily need to be about saying 'I love you' or about 'falling in love'; sex doesn't need to be central and neither does shared couple time or seeing your partner as your most important person in your life.

Real relationships

As well as not reflecting the diversity of relationships across time and culture, rigid ideals about what a 'normal' relationship should look like are also bad for people and their relationships. Psychologist Bjarne M. Holmes found that people who preferred romantic movies, books, and TV programmes tended to believe a set of love myths that actually made their relationships *worse* rather than better. For example, the beliefs that everyone has a 'soulmate' who they are destined to be with and that this partner should be able to 'read our minds', have been linked to relationship difficulties and break-ups.

The ideal of 'The One' perfect partner who will be everything to us is such an unrealistic goal that many people who aspire to it are often unhappy when the reality of life doesn't match up to this fantasy. Some people who buy into this dream end up bouncing from one partner to another as they try to find the non-existent person who has no flaws or shortcomings. Others stay unhappily in relationships that aren't good for them because they fear the stigma of being single or because they convince themselves that this person is 'The One' so they have to stick with them whatever.

It was clear from our study that most people actually *do* question these love myths in all kinds of ways. Most didn't just accept the limited and limiting one-size-fits-all messages; instead they challenged them both explicitly – through what they said about their relationship – and implicitly – through the various different ways of doing relationships which they found worked for them.

Before moving on, we'll just remind you about what we said in each chapter of this book to challenge the idea that there's one way of doing relationships which works for everyone. The ideals of relationships might say the following, but our research found something quite different!

RELATIONSHIP IDEAL: YOU MUST BE IN LOVE WITH EACH OTHER FOREVER.

In Chapter 1 you saw that saying 'I love you' didn't even feature in the top five ways that people liked to feel appreciated; and in Chapter 3 we mentioned that 'being in love' and/or 'being loved' was only the tenth highest thing that people best liked about their relationships. Partners put far more emphasis on demonstrations of kindness and appreciation than they did on declarations of love. Laughing together and friendship also seemed to be valued much more highly than being 'in love'. As Anton and Georgina touched on before, showing love is often prioritised over saying it, particularly through practically supporting each other and sharing chores, for example. Also, many people have had more than one important love relationship in their lives, so they know that love isn't always for ever.

RELATIONSHIP IDEAL: YOU MUST LIVE TOGETHER AND SHARE ALL ASPECTS OF YOUR LIVES.

In Chapter 2 you saw that not all partners live together. Some people choose to live separately and others find ways of living differently due to circumstances which make it difficult to cohabit. Despite the cultural 'relationship escalator', there are many people who find that a good relationship some- times involves getting closer together and sometimes involves moving further apart. For example, in various chapters you've seen how people can find it valuable to make more time for themselves to explore separate interests or to find their own individual spaces in their homes for working, hobbies, or sleeping. Different people also find different ways to share and not-share finances, to go on holiday together or apart, and to combine or separate their friends.

RELATIONSHIP IDEAL: YOU MUSTN'T ARGUE AND YOU MUST ALWAYS KNOW WHAT EACH OTHER WANTS.

In Chapter 3 you saw that conflict is not some terrible sign that things are going wrong. Many partners value arguments – especially small disagreements – because they help to vent tensions rather than let them build up. They also enable them to learn what's important to the other person and so can bring them closer together. Indeed, bickering and teasing are a way of bonding for many people. Also we saw throughout Chapter 3 that people have all different kinds of preferences when it comes to communication. Rather than expecting a partner to know what you want telepathically, it's important to be aware that you'll likely have different communication styles, and to find ways of communicating that work for you which respect this.

RELATIONSHIP IDEAL: YOU MUST HAVE A SEXUAL RELATIONSHIP, KEEP THE PASSION ALIVE, AND REMAIN FAITHFUL TO EACH OTHER.

So many of the myths we hear about sex are wrong and unhelpful. In Chapter 4 we showed that sex isn't necessary for relationship success. Instead, sex can play different roles in different relationships – from being an important and valuable means of connection to being completely unimportant. You saw that people have very different needs in terms of physical affection and that these often fluctuate over time. So it's important that relationships are flexible enough to embrace such changes. Also, throughout the book, you've heard examples of great relationships which are both monogamous and non-monogamous, and that centre solely on the partnership or include other people; so it may be helpful to reconsider what we mean by 'faithful'.

RELATIONSHIP IDEAL: YOU MUST BE THE MOST IMPORTANT PERSON TO EACH OTHER AND MEET ALL OF EACH OTHER'S NEEDS.

In Chapter 5 we knocked the ideal of 'The One' off its pedestal. While partners are certainly important in each other's lives, many people spoke about having additional 'significant others' who were just as – and sometimes even more – important. Throughout the book we've also challenged the idea that partners should meet all of each other's needs. In Chapter 1 you saw that 'me-time' is just as important as 'us-time' for sustaining a relationship; and in Chapter 5 you saw the value that many people place on some third element – whether that is another person, animal, or personal interest. This third element often helps to stabilise the relationship rather than undermining it.

TOP TIP

Pause and think about where you stand on the relationship ideals in the headings above. Are some of them important to you? Do you question some of them?

It's not a matter of discarding them all entirely but rather holding them more lightly and flexibly; thinking about which ones work well for you and which are less helpful.

What is love?

We'll now look in more depth at how people think about love in their relationships. First we'll say a bit more about saying 'I love you', and then we'll turn to the role of friendship and companionship in love relationships.

I Love You

QUIZ TIME: SAYING 'I LOVE YOU'

Think about the place of those three little words in your own relationship:

- Do you ever say 'I love you'?
- If so, who do you say it to?
- What do you mean by it?
- Do you like to hear 'I love you' from a partner?
- Perhaps you like to hear it from other people too, if so who?
- What do you hope they mean by it?

Although, as you've seen, saying 'I love you' wasn't high on the list of what made people feel appreciated or what they liked best in their relationship, it was obviously important to many people that their partner expressed their love in this way:

'Says I love you and means it.'

'We don't express our love to each other any more. It feels weird.'

However it's also clear that 'I love you' has different meanings in different relationships. For some people it reminds them of their ongoing commitment or that they're loved 'warts and all' for the person they are. For others it's something that's said more casually, as a way of saying 'goodbye' on the phone or even to avoid an impending argument. Of course it can also have multiple meanings in the same relationship, depending on how it's said and in what context.

Think about the variety of meanings that love has in the following statements:

'Tells me she loves me and always puts me first.'

'I feel loved for exactly who I am.'

'Nice to have someone who loves you. She makes me feel worthwhile.'

'We love and support each other in all aspects of life.'

'We love and respect each other equally.'

Love can be about knowing that you're 'The One' for your partner or appreciating that they love you and all of your quirks – or we could say 'qualities'! Love can be about feeling useful or being reassured that you'll be supported through difficult times. Love can be linked to fondness, attraction, or respect. In Chapter 1 we saw that people have different love languages, or ways of expressing love, and it also seems that they *mean* different things when they talk of love.

Like Georgina and Anton, many people emphasised the importance of *doing* love as well as saying it, valuing gestures more highly than words, as you saw in Chapter 1. They often described things like cooking, making the bed, and leaving a note for a partner as 'acts of love'. The mutual exchange, 'I love you' and 'I love you too', isn't always verbalised; we also can read it into each other's actions.

> **Jemma:** Dana had left me a tea cup with a teabag, some chocolate and a lovely note. This all made me smile, I love Dana so much.
>
> **Mona:** Told Chloe about Dave's 'risqué' stories and she laughed. I love it when she laughs – it makes my heart float right out of my chest and bob about.

Silent exchanges of 'I love you's' can also be just as important and meaningful as those that are spoken. For Debs and her partner, such silent communication demonstrates their deep understanding and appreciation, and also helps to diffuse otherwise tense situations.

> *'Joss went off to put the kids to bed while I cleared up tea. We usually do it like this – whoever's seen least of the kids puts them to bed. I heard Joss shouting quite a lot. Both kids were sat on the loo sobbing. But then it changed in a flash to messing around and laughing.*
>
> *'That's a familiar routine where the subtext between the adults is 'one of the adults is at the end of their tether and is behaving badly and really needs a break' rather than blaming taking over.*
>
> *'At some point I caught Joss's eye and mouthed 'I love you' to him. He mouthed 'I love you' back to me.'*

Think about the expressions of love that you like to make, and have made to you. Do you like to hear the words, or do you read love into a partner's actions or silences? You might find that you and a partner have different ways of doing this of course.

You're my best friend

Although many people see 'I love you' as the ultimate expression of their feelings for another person, some feel that 'I like you' is actually more profound. The words 'I love you' can lose their meaning over time, especially if people start saying them casually or when they're not really feeling it. For these reasons some people emphasise the importance of friendship in their relationship over love feelings. Where do you stand on this? Is it important that a partner is also your closest friend? Or perhaps you get romantic love and friendship from different people? Or maybe it's something in between?

People who write about love often distinguish between two kinds of love: 'romantic love' and 'companionate love'. Romantic love is the passionate, often sexual, being 'in love' feeling. Companionate love is more about friendship, closeness and fondness. There's sometimes a sense that people move from romantic to companionate love over the course of a relationship, which perhaps explains shifts in sexual desire that can happen over time (see Chapter 3).

Some people see shifts in the experience of love over time as a problem. For example, Monica felt that the loss of romantic love in her relationship meant that she and her partner were now 'friends' and therefore 'not a couple'. Common phrases like 'just friends' and 'more than friends' show how companionate love is often seen as somehow a lesser thing than romantic love.

However the distinctions between these two kinds of love aren't so clear-cut for most people. Many people mix together aspects of romantic and companionate love. They often use terms for each other like 'best friend', 'soul mate', 'lover', 'equal partner', 'parent' and 'companion', often in multiple combinations:

> *'We are best friends as well as lovers.'*
>
> *'I love her. She is my soul mate.'*
>
> *'I love being with her. She is my best friend. She is intelligent and witty and positive. I love her more than I love myself and I love myself a lot.'*

People who emphasise the friendship in their relationships often value being emotionally close and sharing confidences with one another. They also prize mutual support and accepting the other person for all that they are, rather than judging or criticising them. They place special significance on respect, trust and kindness. Some people see this kind of love as *more* important than romantic love: friendship is the major bond in their relationship. For many others there just isn't a clear divide between companionship and romance, and they see their partnership as something which has its own unique energy and intensity. As Debs says:

> 'It's definitely about getting a reflection of yourself back from someone else. It's like two mirrors opposite each other that keep reflecting off each other. I like the image of myself that I see in my partner's response to me, and he likes the image of him that he sees in my response to him.

> 'It's definitely allied to sexual attraction – that's a really important part of it in my mind. It's why talking to him is not like talking to some of my good friends with whom I also share intellectual interests. I don't fancy them, it's just a really interesting conversation, but it hasn't got that kind of energy behind it that talking to him does have.'

The special relationship?

Like saying 'I love you', the idea of being each other's best friend can be both a positive and a negative thing for people. Saying these things can bond partners together, reinforcing their sense of specialness and providing reassurance of their ongoing commitment to *this* relationship. However, as we've seen, it can be very hard if people stop saying these kinds of things over time, or if they start saying them without the actions to back them up. There can also be a pressure to say them when you don't really mean them.

If a partner is the only one that you can say 'I love you' to, or if you expect them to be your 'best' friend, this can also mean that you see the other relationships in your life as less significant. If romantic love is so special, and only available to couples, then how can we make sense of similar feelings towards our children, siblings, parents or lifelong friends? Perhaps instead of putting one kind of relationship on a pedestal it may be helpful to acknowledge all of the different kinds of relationships that sustain us, as we saw in Chapter 5.

You'll probably agree, from what you've read here so far, that love is certainly a slippery concept! It's readily mentioned by some people, and not mentioned at all by others. It's hard to pin down what it means because it differs across relationships, and over time in the same relationship. We'll now turn to this 'time' element as we explore how people tell the stories of their relationships.

Telling our own stories

Going back to that idea of the relationship escalator, we often have an expectation that we've got to meet every marker of a 'successful' relationship at the 'appropriate' time, such as living

---

QUIZ TIME: RELATIONSHIP STORIES

What stories do you tell about your relationships? Think about:

- The stories you tell about the past (e.g., how your relationship started, how it developed, how you got to where you are now).
- The stories you tell about the things that happened which you didn't expect, or the difficult things that happened.
- The stories you tell about the future (e.g., what you want to happen next, how you imagine the long term).

Think about who you tell these stories to – yourself, each other, other people? Are there any stories that you don't tell anyone?

---

together, getting married, and having children. The ideal of living 'happily ever after' can also make us feel that we have to constantly demonstrate how happy we are to the rest of the world. This can make it difficult to admit to the inevitable tough parts of a long-term relationship – both to ourselves and to others.

Past and present

One major way that people celebrate, commit to, and invest in their relationships is through the stories they tell about them. Many people have well-rehearsed stories which they've told many times before about how they got together, for example, a certain holiday they shared, or when their first child was born. You might remember Tony and Sophie's story from Chapter 3, about how they got engaged on a beach in 'windy Wales'!

When we spoke with people in their forties and fifties, they often had stories about how their relationships had changed over time. For example, Moira said:

> *'We don't have to work too hard at it now, because we've been married over 30 years. We knew each other a couple of years before we got married. We met at university in our final year, so we've kind of grown up together really. And I would say in the first five or ten years we probably were working pretty hard at being together and being ourselves: launching our careers and living and everything. So now it's a very nice position to be in when we might have the occasional bicker but that's all it is.'*

For Moira, telling this relationship story was a way of looking back and demonstrating to everyone how all the work they'd put in had paid off. The investment of time and effort created the close, comfortable relationship that they now enjoy.

Other partners in this age group told their relationship stories as a way of distancing themselves from previous relationships which hadn't worked so well. For example, Duncan said:

'I think because we're both second time around, we're very aware of the pitfalls, and things that didn't work in the past. I've learnt a lot since my first marriage.

'I think the biggest thing for me is that my partner lets me be me. I've never had that before. I've always felt that I've – not been forced – but been required to be something that didn't sit well with me.

'So I am very happy with the way things are because of that little allowance that I get just to be me. I say "little allowance", but it's a big thing. I've never had it before, and it's just brilliant.'

When we've had previous long-term relationships, we often bring memories, legacies, and emotional bruises of past lives and loves to our new relationships. It can be useful to look back on the differences between past and current relationships, particularly in relation to how we might do things differently this time round. Lots of people in this situation spoke about learning lessons from the past. People who'd had previous long-term relationships put considerable effort into maintaining their new relationship; perhaps more so than those who hadn't had such experiences. They certainly seem more inclined to appreciate what they have this time around.

People's relationship stories also often take them further back into the past to the relationships that were around them during childhood. You've seen in previous chapters how some people use the homes they grew up in as a model, or yearned for the same kind of pet that they had – or wanted to have – as a child. Others find it important to watch a partner's favourite movies, read their favourite books, or listen to each other's music, in order to 'catch up' on their lives prior to this point.

It also clearly means a lot to some people that partners deliberately create memories to fill the empty spaces of their stories of the past. For example:

TOP TIP

What 'relationships lessons' would you say you've learnt from your life so far? It might be things you've learnt work well or badly in your own relationships, or in those you've seen around you. For example, it could be things like 'if I live with somebody they need to have the same ideas around tidiness that I have', 'we'd need to both want kids', 'I can't be with somebody who lies to me,' 'being with someone who is calm and grounding is actually more important than having lots of things in common', or 'whatever else is going on I need to feel able to be myself.'

Again it's worth holding these lessons a little lightly. They can be helpful, but if they become too rigid they don't work so well because you'll also change over time, and in different relationships.

'I told my partner I wanted a bucket and spade and she made sure she got me a set. Then we all went to the beach so I could build a sandcastle empire! She knows happy memories or lost chances from my childhood mean a lot to me.'

Several people in the research told similar mini-stories about brief moments of escape from their day-to-day lives which were important to them. For example, Sumaira told the following 'adventure' story in her diary, accompanied by this picture.

'I made dinner and my partner came home. It was lovely to see him. We had a hug and chatted about our day. He got changed then we ate at the table together and I loved it so much. It's perfect – just us and food. What more could I want? After dinner he put a song on he likes and we danced, which was funny. Then we went for a walk. It was beautiful. We got lost and walked through grass which was taller than me and I got scared that it might get dark. We found our way through – it just took a while! It was really nice – certainly an adventure.'

When the going gets tough

Stressful events happen in all relationships. In our research we asked whether people had been through any of the major recognised life stressors in the past two years. We found that around a third of them had moved house and a similar proportion had started an educational course. Around a quarter had lost a job, a similar proportion had started a new job, and a similar proportion had been through a bereavement. Many people had experienced far more than one or two of these stressors over the last two years.

We know from research that relationships come under immense pressure at times of transition and stress, and that

TRY IT YOURSELF: RELATIONSHIP STORIES

Decide on a relationship story that you'd like to tell and find a way of telling it so that it will last. It might be a story from a current relationship with a partner or friend, or one from the past.

You could pick the whole sweep of your relationship or the story of how you met, the story of a key event in your life, the story of a certain mini-adventure or the story of a 'perfect day' that you shared together.

Think creatively about how you'd to tell the story. You could write it down if you like writing, or you could record yourself telling it. You could create a scrap book to tell the tale, including a selection of photographs (in an album or on your computer) or drawings like Sumaira's. You could create a memory box of objects that relate to the story. You could imagine the relationship as a book or a computer game and say what the different chapter headings, or levels, would be. Anything that works for you is fine.

You can share the story with your partner or with somebody in your life who doesn't know it already. If it's a story from your current relationship, you could both try telling the same story in your own ways and then sharing them. Sharing your stories and re-living the experience can add another chapter to the story itself.

these kinds of things can contribute to relationship breakdown. However, we also found that the opposite was true. Going through something difficult together can help to strengthen a relationship. In fact, people who'd been through several stressful events actually scored higher on relationship satisfaction and put more effort into maintaining their relationship.

This reminds us that emotional 'ups and downs' and changes in life circumstances are a part of all relationships, to different degrees and at different points in time. Rather than stretching the relationship to breaking point, stressful times can actually consolidate it, with partners pulling together and being there for each other through difficulties and heartache. Surviving adversities and finding a way to tell a shared story through the experience seems to make all the difference.

One powerful example of this came from Debs, who you might remember from Chapter 2 where she described losing her baby. Here she tells more of the story of how her partner's ways of commemorating their loss helped her to appreciate him, and their relationship, even more.

'When we lost the baby we decided that we wanted to do something symbolic, a kind of grieving ceremony. We invited just a few very closest family and friends and we'd already decided to plant a tree.

'I think most of the ideas came from him. I mean we did ask people to suggest things. But the actual symbolic acts: that was nearly all Joss. And I just feel so blessed. It feels like such a gift from Joss when he can do that. Particularly because I don't expect him to do it. That was really meaningful. I said "You're really good at this" and he said "Yes, I am aren't I? It's really surprising."'

A more everyday kind of stress that happens to us fairly regularly is illness. Many people talked about how important acts of kindness during periods of illness were, such as a partner bringing them soup, a hot-water bottle, or a pet to cuddle. More major illnesses often became a focal point of relationship stories because, like losing a baby, they create a gap between the expected relationship story and what actually happened. For example, Lucy and Garry told the story of when Lucy broke both her arms and Garry had to take over all her domestic roles, as well as dressing and caring for her, for the nine weeks that she wore plaster casts.

Lucy: It was very stressful. It was very, very frustrating for me.
Garry: I have to say I didn't feel particularly stressed about it. It just happened and you've got to get on with it so we did.

Lucy: I was just anxious the whole time that I was asking too much, and then I had to ask for this, that and the other to be done. It wasn't a good time.

Garry: It was all right and we got through it and it wasn't for ever.

Lucy: That's the thing that you focus on. There's people out there that aren't getting better. At least my wrists were going to get better. But I didn't want to put extra burden on Garry and stress Garry out.

Garry: I think I felt okay. I don't recall getting too irritated about anything, did I?

Lucy: Well, you didn't seem best pleased some of the time!

Garry: It did tire me out a bit at times. And you know what I'm like when I'm tired, I get a bit irritated. It's a really bad habit of mine, when I see somebody injure themselves initially there's not a great deal of sympathy from me because that's the way they used to operate in the navy. If you had a broken arm, they'd give you an aspirin, figuratively speaking, until they realised, 'Oh, okay, it is broken' or whatever. So it's an old habit dying hard, and I should have been better because you are my wife.

Lucy: I think we learnt a few lessons from it and I like to think that we are a stronger couple because it proves that we can get through times when things are tough.

In this example we can see how Garry and Lucy navigate wanting to tell somewhat different stories through what happened. Garry seems drawn to the 'it was fine, you've just got to get on with it' story. Lucy, however, needs to tell the story of how hard it was for her to have to rely so much on Garry, and how *his* struggle to deal with it all impacted negatively on her. The back and forth between them, when their stories conflict, leads Garry to recognise that his past experiences might mean that he isn't terribly sympathetic around illness. Once he's woven the past in with the present in this way, Lucy can move them into the future by saying – as so many people did – that going through this tough time together proves the strength of their relationship.

Hopefully this shows you that partners' stories don't always have to be perfectly in sync in order to be valuable for the relationship. Think about the stories that you tell through the tough times – separately and together – and whether telling stories helps you to make sense of things or to strengthen the relationship.

Where do we go from here?

One more key element of how people tell their relationship stories is when they project their relationship into the future. Stories of imagined futures can also help us through stressful periods.

Imagined futures

When people deal with the tough times they often look to what you might call the 'relationship horizon'. They're walking along a rough path together, but they can look along the road to where it smoothens out, or up to the peaceful hills in the distance, and that can help them to keep going.

For example, you might remember, in Chapter 4, how Louise and Luke spoke about the tough time they were having. Luke was working long hours, Louise felt the burden of child-care, and had withdrawn from sex with Luke because she was so unhappy with the imbalance in their relationship and in her life more generally. One way they dealt with this was by imagining the future when these pressures were no longer there. Sometimes the relationship horizon was far away, such as imagining when Luke got a new job, or when the children grew up. Sometimes it was just around the corner, such as an upcoming child-free mini-break, or some snatched time together over the weekend.

Luke: I'm just really looking forward to next couple of months. I finish my course and then things get a little bit easier than they have been. I always said they were going to be difficult this year and it has been a particularly difficult year. But it is soon easing.

Louise: It is tough him being out of work: doing the course and things like that. We have a future, but it just depends on how long it's going to take to get there. But hopefully it will be this year, which will be nice.

You can see from this example that the following things are helpful in imagining the future:

- Having a shared vision of the future
- Having known that the difficult period was coming up beforehand
- Having some idea how long the tough time is going to last – ideally not too long!

When problems are long term and uncertain, it can be helpful to create multiple mini-horizons to focus on, for example after a doctor's appointment there might be a clearer picture of an illness, or you might strive to get the next job application submitted rather than focusing on getting the job itself.

People also often use the past to prepare them for the future. For example, remember Debs' analogy from Chapter 1, of putting deposits in the bank of their relationship during the good times in order to see them through times that might be more tricky further down the line.

Other people use experiences from their own childhoods as a kind of 'biographical anchor' to tether their own relationships, giving them a story for how they'll maintain the relationship into the future. For example:

'My dream is getting married and then we'd be the old couple, like my nan and granddad, sat in the garden holding hands, sipping flat lemonade.'

You can also think back to Chapter 2, and how people built their relationship stories into the bricks and mortar of their own homes. For example, Debs described how finding the 'right house' helped her and Joss to weather the storm of losing their baby. Anna pictured her future 'ideal home' to imagine how her relationship would strengthen and develop.

In her diary, Hayley similarly described using her garden to nurture her relationship and to ensure that it grew in the future.

'I went downstairs and made breakfast for us, which we ate in the garden. Since moving in last October we have worked hard on making the garden nice. We tour the garden together every day to see how things are: veggies growing, chickens happy, plants taken, etc. We do this while talking about our plans for the future.'

TOP TIP

If you're having a tough time in any area at the moment, try thinking through the following things to create your own imagined future.

Close relationship horizons: What are the things coming up soon that will ease things, at least for a little while? If there aren't any already happening could you create some, like an evening off, or getting a little support with reaching a short-term goal?

Further-away relationship horizons: What are the points further away when the difficulty will ease or end entirely? Again if this isn't clear you might build in things deliberately like a trip away, or doing a short course that could give you some skills with how to deal with whatever's going on.

Shared vision: If you have a partner – or other people are involved – do you have a shared vision of the future? If so perhaps you can spend some time together imagining it. It can help to build in several variations that would work for you (so that it doesn't become one target that you have to meet otherwise you'll feel bad). If your visions for the future are different, then some of the ideas in Chapter 3 could help you to communicate about this, finding the areas you share and the places where you differ, and how to accommodate both.

Preparation: It helps to know when difficulties are coming. Are there elements of this tough time that you can predict? If so you can make some plans around them in advance so that it feels a bit more doable. For example, this person can help me out with this part of the problem, this week is free enough for me to get that bit done.

Timing: Everything ends eventually – do you have a sense of when this difficulty will pass? If that is uncertain maybe you can focus on points at which some aspect of it will be over. For example, by the end of the year we'll have a clearer picture about this aspect; over the holidays this person will be around who can support us with it.

The past: Think back to when you've been through tough times before. Remember that these times show you that you can weather the storm, and that nothing lasts forever. What got you through those times? Could you apply some of those things here?

Anchors: What aspects of your home, or other places you spend time in, could help to tether you while this is going on? For example is there somewhere you can go every day for a little bit of peace away from the tough stuff? Is there something that you can do at home that helps to ground you?

Sharing stories of the past, present, and future, is one of the things that many people like best about their relationships. Stories connect us together and give us an emotionally meaningful way of making sense of our lives.

'Shared history and commitment to a shared future.'

'We have shared wonderful memories.'

We can take a lot of pleasure in pausing for reflection, and appreciating what we have in this way. Marking specific points every year is one way of remembering and continuing our stories. This might include formal relationship markers like anniversaries, or private memories and times that have specific meanings to us. Remember the person in Chapter 1 who brought his partner the first orange rose from his garden every year?

On the last page of their research diary, Kim and Freda projected their relationship from the present memories they'd been sharing into the future. They wrote *'The End (but not of Kim and Freda who will go on for ever – even after death)'*, and drew this picture of themselves and their cats.

Building a relationship support system

We've seen that it can be hard to tell the whole stories of our relationships when we get such powerful messages about the importance of living 'happily ever after', 'keeping up appearances' and not admitting to anything which seems like a 'failure'.

People can end up feeling very isolated in their relationships if they only feel able to tell 'positive' stories to the rest of the world, or if they feel that some aspects of their relationship have to be kept under wraps. At worst, some people remain in damaging and abusive relationships because they feel unable to tell anybody what's going on. More generally there's often a sense that relationships should be 'private'. This can mean that people don't seek support when they're having tough times, and they don't have a chance to check out with somebody else whether their partner's behaviour is okay or not.

For these reasons it's worth thinking about the support systems which might be available to your relationship. Is it easier to be yourself around certain people in your family, friendship group or community than others? Do you and your partner have at least one other person who you can talk with openly about your relationship? Is there anybody whose advice you can trust in times of trouble? Are there ways to get some air flowing through the relationship regularly so that you can keep reflecting on it, rather than getting stuck in how it's 'always been'?

Some people find it useful to have a weekend away with a close friend once a year, where they look at their whole life from a distance. Such time out can have personal benefits and it can also give you a renewed appreciation of what's working well in your relationship and also areas where you'd like to make some changes.

Support from other people can be emotional, practical or both. For example, when Lucy told the story of her broken arms it was clear that her wider network of friends were vital to her:

Think about your own relationship support system by answering the same questions that we asked in our survey.

QUIZ TIME: RELATIONSHIP SUPPORT SYSTEMS

1. Would you consider turning to any of the following for support, help or advice with your relationship?

Please tick only one box

Health Visitor   GP   Relationship therapy   Individual therapy
Websites   Solicitor   Religious community   Agony aunts/ uncles None

Other _____

2. Have you made use of any of the above for relationship support in the past?

No   Yes

If yes, which?

_____

3. If yes, was this
Helpful   Unhelpful   Other _____

4. Why do you say this?

5. Do you talk about your relationship to any of the following people? (tick as many as apply)

My child/ren Parent Sibling   Colleagues   My partner
Religious   community Friend/s   Other family members
Neighbours   I don't talk to anybody about it

Other _____

'We were very lucky that we had other people that came and help, didn't we? There were people knocking on the door, people who cooked dinner for us, and other people helped with the school run. We were very lucky.'

This is what we found when we looked at people's answers to these kinds of questions.

VITAL STATISTICS:

Help Seeking and Advice

People spoke about a diverse range of sources of advice and support. However, just under a quarter of them said that they wouldn't turn to any form of support if they were struggling in their relationship.

The most popular source of support that people mentioned was therapy, and many of them said they'd prefer to go to a relationship therapist than to an individual counsellor, somebody who could work with them together. This can often be more valuable than a one-to-one therapist if the problem is a relationship difficulty.

Around one in ten people used websites for support including those provided by relationship organisations like www. relate.org.uk and www.oneplusone.org.uk. Many people find that support forums like www.mumsnet.com, www.dadtalk. co.uk and www.netmums.com help them to manage the often tricky balance between parenting and partnering. Such sites give different perspectives or topic-focused advice rather than help from any one relationship 'expert'. Group forums often include contributions from people who've been through similar things and it's possible to remain anonymous more easily. However, people tend to be less objective and to talk from their personal experience on these kinds of forums – so it's worth bearing this in mind when you read the advice.

Finally, help-seeking remains quite gendered. Men are generally less likely than women to get relationship support, including talking to friends and family about their problems. This may be due to the social pressures on men to be strong and rational rather than vulnerable and emotional. Some men in our research did find it helpful to confide in people outside their relationship. Fathers were the least likely group to access support and advice if they were struggling in their relationships.

As well as conversations about how you like to communicate (Chapter 3), express love (Chapter 1), or connect physically (Chapter 4), it can be useful in a relationship to have a conversation – ideally early on – about the support systems that you already have. It can be reassuring to know that your partner will be able to get support from other people rather than turning only to you. When the difficulty is with the relationship it's particularly important that you have other people around to support you, because supporting a partner when the problem is about you is a very big ask and not something that most of us can manage!

It might be that you have different ideas about how private, or open, people should be about their relationships. For example, talking to a friend about sexual problems in your relationship may feel like a breach of trust to one of you. This doesn't mean that you shouldn't talk about these areas of your life, but it can be helpful to talk about who you'd talk to, and how personal these conversations may get, *before* any such conversations happen.

If you drew a picture of the significant people in your life at the end of Chapter 5 this could be a helpful place to start thinking about the people who might offer support. You could think about whether there are some people who support your relationship, and other people who support you separately – as individuals.

It can also be useful to think about whether you'd turn to somebody neutral if you were struggling and who that would be. Certainly relationship therapists and counsellors can be a good source of help and advice. However, it's important to remember that they vary in quality just like any professional.

Don't go to the first person you come across online. Try and get recommendations. Shop around just as you would for a plumber! The important thing with relationship therapy is that you each feel understood by the therapist. Also, if you're in a same-sex relationship, a non-monogamous relationship, or a relationship within a particular religious community, it's worth finding a therapist who is already familiar with those things so that you don't end up having to educate them!

Of course counselling isn't for everyone. Some people find support groups or community events about relationships more helpful than counselling. Friends or online support can feel more safe and reciprocal. It's important to find the kinds of support that best suit you.

Conclusions (to this chapter)

In this chapter we've explored how we tell our own love stories between and beyond the stories that are circulating around us all the time: in our families and communities, and in the media and popular culture.

SUMMARY SUGGESTIONS:
YOUR LOVE STORY

Here are a few more things to try yourself, based on this chapter.

- Think about the commitments you'd like to make to a partner, or have made to you, away from the ones that we generally hear about, like wedding ceremonies. What would you like to promise and have promised? Consider how these might change over the course of your relationship.
- How do you let your partner know that you love them? Is it about words and/or deeds? Make a time to express love to your partner. Notice how it feels.

- Reflect on your childhood. Are there particularly happy memories which you could take into your current relationship? Are there things that you didn't get as a child that you could create now? Whether it's going to the seaside, baking a cake, or building a cushion fort, make a time to bring a childish thing into your adult life with a partner.

- What are your relationship markers? Maybe you always celebrate a certain anniversary or special day? Think of a less obvious way that you might regularly mark a relationship and how you could go about doing it. Is there an event which on the surface appears quite inconsequential but that has a special meaning for you and your partner? Is there something you could do that's different to the usual cards, gifts or holidays?

- Make some time with your partner to draw out your relationship support systems on a big sheet of paper. Include all the mutual, and separate, people, animals and things in your lives that support each of you, and your relationship. Then add – in a different colour perhaps – additional ones that you'd like to put in place in the future.

- Try writing your own relationship story, as suggested in the 'try it yourself' box earlier in this chapter. You can first write the relationship story that you grew up with: the expectations and messages that you received about how your relationship should be. Consider the ways in which your story followed this and the ways that it differed. How can you embrace your own journey in all of its twists and turns, instead of comparing it against other stories?

Conclusions (to the book)

So we've reached the end of the book! We hope you enjoyed meeting all the people who've shared their experiences and expertise with you along the way: the relationship researchers and writers of course, but – see after more than them – the everyday people who told us their stories and the lessons they've learnt about love.

You've also learnt a lot about your own relationships on this journey. You've learnt that there's no one-size-fits-all secret to enduring love and that *you* are the expert on your own relationship. You've learnt that love comes in all shapes and sizes, each with their own kind of beauty and challenges. You've certainly learnt about the vital importance of the cup of tea (or your equivalent, whatever that is)!

So what can you take away from this journey to your own relationships? What *are* those elusive secrets to enduring love?

The secrets of enduring love

DIFFERENT THINGS FOR DIFFERENT RELATIONSHIPS

There's no one secret for enduring love but many secrets. Diversity is the only rule and what works for one relationship won't necessarily work for another. Different people prefer different expressions of love, intimacy, and appreciation; they need different kinds of shared and separate time; they communicate, and resolve conflict in different ways; and they work better in different kinds of living situations and relationship structures. Love, sex, home and family have different meanings to different people and their importance shifts and changes over the course of a relationship. We know that saying that different things work for different people might not sound like a revelation! But it's remarkable how many people think they have to do what 'everybody else' does, rather than finding their own way. We can't stress enough how crucial this understanding is to enduring love.

GET THE SMALL STUFF RIGHT AND THE BIG STUFF FOLLOWS

'Relationship work' often happens in the minutiae and mundanities of everyday life. It's the quick message, the word of thanks, or the spontaneous dance in the living room – rather than the big commitments, deep conversations, or major celebrations – that really matter. Make some relationship rituals of your own to connect you to each other. Whether you live together or apart, it's about making your relationship feel like home.

MAKE TIME: TOGETHER AND SEPARATE

It's so important to build shared moments into our busy lives. People love cooking together, having a laugh, grabbing a quick cuddle, or collapsing together in front of the TV. It's also just as important to get time out of a relationship to nurture ourselves and the 'significant others' that support our relationships. Make sure you have some daily and weekly us-time and me-time, whatever works for you. In our culture, with its focus on 'getting things done', this can be seen as 'unproductive', but caring for yourself and your relationships gives an invaluable foundation to pretty much everything else.

FIND YOUR OWN STORY

It's all about finding your own story, rather than trying to force your relationship into the love stories that you've heard in the world around you. You've seen that relationships don't need to be sexual or cohabiting in order to work well; that sometimes *not* communicating is the most effective form of communication; and that arguments, transitions and stressful times can strengthen rather than weaken a relationship. Relationships are often about more than two people – in all kinds of ways; and some relationships that last a short time can be more 'successful' than ones that last a lifetime. It's vital to be able to tell your own relationship stories instead of feeling pressured to show some perfect 'happily ever after' to the rest of the world.

So please own your own relationship story. Like the people in this book you might even want to share it with others: maybe they'll learn something!

FURTHER READING AND RESOURCES

Here are a few of the books that we've mentioned over the course of the book, along with a few others which you might find useful for thinking about these things further. Most of them also have companion websites which we've included here as well.

Barker, M. (2013). *Rewriting the rules: An integrative guide to love, sex and relationships*. London: Routledge. (www.rewriting-the-rules.com)

Barker, M. J. & Hancock, J. (2016). *Enjoy Sex (How, when and if you want to): A practical and inclusive guide*. London: Icon Books. (www.senseaboutsex.com)

Chapman, G. (2010). *The five love languages: The secret to love that lasts*. Chicago, IL: Northfield Publishing. (www.5lovelanguages.com)

Coontz, S. (2005). *Marriage, a history*. New York, NY: Penguin. (www.stephaniecoontz.com)

Dubberley, E. (2013). *Garden of desires*. London: Black Lace. (www.dubberley.com)

Figes, K. (2010). *Couples: The truth*. London: Virago. (www.katefiges.co.uk)

Friedman, J. (2011). *What you really really want*. Berkeley, CA: Seal Press. (www.jaclynfriedman.com)

Gottman, J. & Silver, N. (2012). *What makes love last*. New York, NY: Simon & Schuster. (www.gottman.com)

Lerner, H. (2003). *The dance of intimacy*. New York, NY: William Morrow Paperbacks. (www.harrietlerner.com)

Lerner, H. (2004). *The dance of anger: A woman's guide to changing the patterns of intimate relationships*. New York, NY: Element. (www.harrietlerner.com)

Neustatter, A. (2012). *A home for the heart: 11 ideas to balance your life*. London: Gibson Square Books.

Penny, L. (2011). *Meat market: Female flesh under capitalism*. London: Zero Books. (www.laurie-penny.com)

Perel, E. (2007). *Mating in captivity: Sex, lies and domestic bliss*. London: Hodder & Stoughton. (www.estherperel.com).

Tavris, C. & Aronson, E. (2008). *Mistakes were made (but not by me)*. London: Pinter & Martin. (www.caroltavris.com)

Veaux, F. & Rickert, E. (2014). *More than two*. Thorntree Press. (www.morethantwo.com)

Welwood, J. (2006). *Perfect love imperfect relationships*. Boston, MA: Trumpeter. (www.johnwelwood.com)

If you're interested in the more academic book about the project, here are the details:

Gabb, J. & Fink, J. (2015). *Couple relationships in the 21st century*. Basingstoke: Palgrave Macmillan.

You can read more about the project, including a list of organisations who work with relationships in the UK, on our project website: www.open.ac.uk/researchprojects/enduringlove

APPENDIX: THE 36 QUESTIONS[1]

Block 1

1. Given the choice of anyone in the world, whom would you want as a dinner guest?
2. Would you like to be famous? In what way?
3. Before making a phone call, do you ever rehearse what you're going to say? Why?
4. What would constitute a perfect day for you?
5. When did you last sing to yourself? To someone else?
6. If you were able to live to the age of 90 and retain either the mind or body of a 30-year-old for the last 60 years of your life, which would you choose?
7. Do you have a secret hunch about how you will die?
8. Name three things you and your partner appear to have in common.
9. For what in your life do you feel most grateful?
10. If you could change anything about the way you were raised, what would it be?
11. Take four minutes and tell you partner your life story in as much detail as possible.
12. If you could wake up tomorrow having gained one quality or ability, what would it be?

Block 2

13. If a crystal ball could tell you the truth about yourself, your life, the future or anything else, what would you want to know?
14. Is there something that you've dreamt of doing for a long time? Why haven't you done it?

[1] From: Aron, A., Melinat, E., Aron, E. N., Vallone, R. D., & Bator, R. J. (1997). The experimental generation of interpersonal closeness: A procedure and some preliminary findings. *Personality and Social Psychology Bulletin*, 23(4), 363–377.

15. What is the greatest accomplishment of your life?
16. What do you value most in a friendship?
17. What is your most treasured memory?
18. What is your most terrible memory?
19. If you knew that in one year you would die suddenly, would you change anything about the way you are now living? Why?
20. What does friendship mean to you?
21. What roles do love and affection play in your life?
22. Alternate sharing something you consider a positive characteristic of your partner. Share a total of five items.
23. How close and warm is your family? Do you feel your childhood was happier than most other people's?
24. How do you feel about your relationship with your mother?

Block 3

25. Make three true 'we' statements each. For instance, 'we are both in this room feeling...'
26. Complete this sentence 'I wish I had someone with whom I could share...'
27. If you were going to become a close friend with your partner, please share what would be important for him or her to know.
28. Tell your partner what you like about them: be honest this time, saying things that you might not say to someone you've just met.
29. Share with your partner an embarrassing moment in your life.
30. When did you last cry in front of another person? By yourself?
31. Tell your partner something that you like about them already.
32. What, if anything, is too serious to be joked about?
33. If you were to die this evening with no opportunity to communicate with anyone, what would you most regret not having told someone? Why haven't you told them yet?
34. Your house, containing everything you own, catches fire. After saving your loved ones and pets, you have time to safely make a final dash to save any one item. What would it be? Why?
35. Of all the people in your family, whose death would you find most disturbing? Why?
36. Share a personal problem and ask your partner's advice on how he or she might handle it. Also, ask your partner to reflect back to you how you seem to be feeling about the problem you have chosen.